D0731936

THE **STRUCTURED** INTERVIEW

PRESSES DE L'UNIVERSITÉ DU QUÉBEC
Le Delta I, 2875, boulevard Laurier, bureau 450
Québec (Québec) G1V 2M2
Téléphone : (418) 657-4399 • Télécopieur : (418) 657-2096
Courriel : puq@puq.ca • Internet : www.puq.ca

Diffusion / Distribution :

CANADA et autres pays

PROLOGUE INC.
1650, boulevard Lionel-Bertrand (Québec) J7H 1N7
Téléphone : (450) 434-0306 / 1 800 363-2864

FRANCE
AFPU-DIFFUSION
SODIS

BELGIQUE
PATRIMOINE SPRL
168, rue du Noyer
1030 Bruxelles
Belgique

SUISSE
SERVIDIS SA
5, rue des Chaudronniers,
CH-1211 Genève 3
Suisse

THE STRUCTURED INTERVIEW

Normand Pettersen – André Durivage

ENHANCING STAFF SELECTION

2008

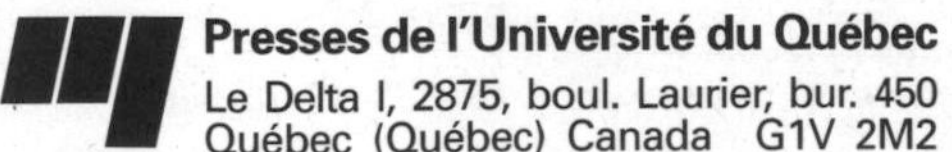

Presses de l'Université du Québec
Le Delta I, 2875, boul. Laurier, bur. 450
Québec (Québec) Canada G1V 2M2

Bibliothèque et Archives nationales du Québec
and Library and Archives Canada cataloguing in publication

Pettersen, Normand

The structured interview: enhancing staff selection

ISBN 978-2-7605-1537-6

1. Employment interviewing. 2. Employee selection. I. Durivage, André, 1956- . II. Title.

HF5549.5.I6P47 2008 658.3'1124 C2007-942227-6

Nous reconnaissons l'aide financière du gouvernement du Canada par l'entremise du Programme d'aide au développement de l'industrie de l'édition (PADIE) pour nos activités d'édition.

La publication de cet ouvrage a été rendue possible grâce à l'aide financière de la Société de développement des entreprises culturelles (SODEC).

Révision linguistique : LOUIS COURTEAU

Mise en pages : INFOSCAN COLLETTE QUÉBEC

Couverture : RICHARD HODGSON

1 2 3 4 5 6 7 8 9 PUQ 2008 9 8 7 6 5 4 3 2 **1**

Dépôt légal – 1er trimestre 2008
Bibliothèque et Archives nationales du Québec / Bibliothèque et Archives Canada
Imprimé au Canada

CONTENTS

THE SELECTION INTERVIEW PROCESS 19

STEP 4

STEP 5

LIST OF TABLES

LIST OF FIGURES

ACKNOWLEDGMENTS

A book is rarely the product of its authors alone, and this one is no exception. We would like to thank all the people who each in their own way helped us so generously.

In particular, we thank Hélène Guévin, Gilbert Guindon and Stéphane Migneault, at the Quebec Secrétariat du Conseil du trésor, for their advice and comments while we were writing a training module on the selection interview, the real starting point for this book. Diane Lambert-Tesolin, from the Quebec Ministère des Services gouvernementaux, deserves special praise for her remarkable editing skills. Manon Geoffroy and Marc-André Verrette, consultants at Groupe ressources (DGO), and Jean Fortin, consultant at ANCIA, methodically revised the first complete version of the manuscript. Spurred on by their comments and the discussions that followed, we wrote a second version. Gilles Lajoie, consultant, then carefully examined and questioned practically every section of the new manuscript. We have benefited a great deal from his ideas, which were always constructive. Just before going to press, Claude Guindon, an industrial/organizational psychologist at Hydro-Québec's Human Resources Directorate, made judicious remarks on the final manuscript. The employees at Évaluation Personnel Sélection International (EPSI) helped strengthen the practical aspects of the book with their pertinent comments and professional expertise, especially with the exercises and the guide to formulating questions. The team of advisors at the Mouvement Desjardins, particularly Hélène Boileau, Jocelyne Goyer and Philippe Reitz (now with the Quebec Commission de la santé et de la sécurité au travail), ardent supporters of the structured interview, allowed us to refine several of the approaches and methods presented in this book. Nor can we forget the team at Presses de l'Université du Québec, who are real artisans, motivated by the ideal of quality work. To all these people we offer a heartfelt thank you.

Normand Pettersen is grateful to and proud of his children, Géraldine and Renaud, whose maturity gave him the peace of mind so essential for an author. André Durivage thanks his spouse, Julie Thibault, for her support and her wise professional advice on the use of structured interviews. He also thanks his three children, Gabriel, Joël and Pascale, for their support, love and patience.

INTRODUCTION

The interview is the most frequently employed tool for selecting personnel; almost every organization uses them. Because recruiters consider interviews are more reliable for hiring decisions, they place more confidence in the interview than any other means of selection.

Over the years, many authors have tried to explain the popularity of the interview.[1] First of all, most managers and other decision makers think that by the end of an interview, they can evaluate candidates' characteristics and abilities and know whether they meet the job requirements. A large number of managers are further convinced that the interview is the best way to evaluate a candidate, even though

1. Dipboye (1992); Taylor and O'Driscoll (1995).

they recognize the virtues of more objective tools such as tests. They think it essential to meet candidates face to face to make a judgment on their qualifications. Besides, managers and employers usually like conducting interviews, especially meeting the candidate in person. In any event, candidates see the interview as an opportunity to demonstrate their qualifications. Whatever the reason, the interview has clearly become standard in the organization and it is taken for granted that there can be no selection without an interview.

In contrast to other methods of evaluation, the interview is not only used to evaluate. It can be a way of recruiting candidates, pointing out the organization's strengths, or the first step in socializing future employees. It may also be that the interview is used to control the selection process. It is true that the interview's flexibility gives managers the opportunity to establish and consolidate their influence over the choice of future employees, whereas more objective, even mechanical methods, such as psychometric tests, reduce this influence.

Purpose and contents of this book. Since the selection interview is the employers' preferred tool for choosing their staff, it is crucial to maximize its effectiveness by using tested techniques and preparing interviewers appropriately. This book presents the most recent knowledge and techniques in the field of the selection interview. It is a practical guide that recognizes the many constraints in the organizational world. Rather than proposing a single approach, a recipe that applies to every situation, this guide instead offers various ways of conducting an interview, each with their advantages and limitations, so that the appropriate interview for each situation can be chosen intelligently. Of course, this versatility requires more judgment and effort on the part of interviewers, therefore more time. However, all we need to convince us that such an investment is required is to think of the consequences of one bad hiring decision that could be disastrous for the organization and its entire staff.[2]

2. See Pettersen (2000), Chapter 1.

The selection interview consists of a conversation with a candidate to obtain information on his or her ability to carry out the duties involved in a given job. Interviews can be used at different stages of the selection process.

a) *At the beginning of the process*: A brief **pre-selection** interview may be held to ensure that the person is sufficiently qualified to be a candidate for the position. Sometimes this interview is also used to attract the candidates who seem most appropriate.

b) *During the process*: One or more **in-depth** interviews are usually conducted to precisely evaluate the candidate's knowledge, skills and other qualities in relation to the job requirements.

c) *At the end of the process*: The **hiring** interview is often the last step. It is useful for offering the job to the best candidate and for discussing the arrangements for bringing him or her into the organization.

The knowledge and techniques presented here primarily relate to the in-depth interview. Drawing on numerous research studies, we first outline the advantages of the structured interview over the traditional interview too often favoured by organizations. We follow with detailed explanations of what has to be done at each of the six steps that make up the structured interview process: 1) conducting a job analysis, 2) determining the selection criteria and the rules for making decisions, 3) creating the interview guide, 4) conducting the interview, 5) evaluating the candidates, and 6) making the hiring decision.

THE STRUCTURED JOB-RELATED INTERVIEW DEFINED

Before we can judge the success of a selection interview and choose the best techniques, we must first determine what makes for an effective interview. An interview can be considered effective on the basis of four main criteria: 1) validity, 2) reliability, 3) compliance with the law and the organization's policies, as well as legal defensibility, and 4) candidates' reaction.[1]

CRITERIA FOR THE EFFECTIVENESS OF THE SELECTION INTERVIEW

1. *Validity.* Validity is the most important quality of a measurement instrument – its ability to measure what it is supposed to measure, or predict what it is supposed to predict. In personnel selection, a valid interview makes it possible to find the best candidates for a given position. In other words, the validity of an instrument is verified when the interviewers' evaluations predict candidates' future performance adequately and without bias (e.g., without prejudice based on sex or race, favouritism, etc.).

   Validity is therefore defined by the relationship that exists between the results obtained by the candidates in the interview and their job performance once they have been hired. This relationship between the measurement instrument and performance is usually quantified using a statistical index, the correlation coefficient (in this context, called the criterion-related validity coefficient), whose absolute value varies between 0.00 and 1.00. The higher the validity, the higher the coefficient.

2. *Reliability.* Reliability is related to the precision, or constancy of results obtained with a measuring instrument. Basically, a reliable result is not distorted by random events (e.g., a candidate's momentary indisposition, an ambiguous question variously interpreted by different candidates, or varying behaviours of different interviewers during the course of the interviews).[2] In the case of a selection interview, reliability takes the form of stability, which can be verified in two ways:

---

1. Campion, Palmer and Campion (1997); Eder and Harris (1999); Pettersen (2000).
2. Without reliability, validity is not possible. Reliability is a necessary but not sufficient condition of validity.

a) Stability of evaluations *from one interviewer to another* – if two or more interviewers evaluate the same candidate, their evaluations should be similar.

b) Stability of evaluations *from one interview to another*: if the same interviewer evaluates two equivalent candidates, the evaluations should be equivalent.

Reliability is often the focus of litigation. Candidates might contest their evaluation, attesting that they were not given the same questions or treated the same way by interviewers, for example, or that identical responses by different candidates led to different evaluations.

3. *Compliance with the law and the organization's policies, as well as legal defensibility.* The selection interview used for hiring or promotion purposes must proceed within the limits of a formal framework. If the interview becomes the subject of a dispute, the appellants' allegations must be responded to and evidence that the law or regulation in question was complied with must be produced. Although each case is different, the validity and reliability of the interview will become decisive issues. These legal considerations are another important criterion of the effectiveness of the selection interview, because in many Western countries, selection practices are subject to various laws, policy statements or contractual agreements.

4. *The candidates' reactions.* It is desirable that the candidates have a positive perception of the interview to avoid harmful consequences to the work atmosphere, the reputation of the organization or its recruiting power. In addition, the candidate's perception of the interview will be instrumental in his or her decision to mount a legal challenge or take a case before the appropriate tribunal. The candidate's attitude can be influenced by any number of factors including: *a*) the relevance of the questions, *b*) the professionalism and respect shown by the interviewers, and *c*) the candidate's own perception of the fairness of the process.

Now that the criteria for effectiveness have been established, we can look at the kind of interview discussed in this book – the structured job-related interview. Over the years, several hundred empirical studies must have been done on the selection interview.[3] The invaluable data they have produced have made it possible to establish a set of best practices. Among these best practices, two are obvious: structuring the components of the interview and focusing them on the job to be filled.

THE STRUCTURED INTERVIEW: CHARACTERISTICS AND ADVANTAGES

The more standardized the components of an interview are, the more structured the interview. The degree of structure of an interview will vary mainly following the two outstanding components of standardization:[4]

a) The degree to which the **questions** are standardized. Some interviewers allow themselves a lot of leeway in the questions they ask candidates and the way they ask them. Other interviewers, however, insist on asking exactly the same questions in the same way in the same order. Obviously, between these two extremes, various degrees of standardization can be used.

b) The degree to which the **procedures used to evaluate** the information obtained and the worth of the candidate are standardized. The least standardization occurs when the procedure has not been defined and the interviewers are free to choose the method for arriving at a sound decision, most often qualitatively (e.g., this candidate is very good). On the other hand, maximum standardization occurs when a strict procedure requires the interviewers to provide a quantitative evaluation of a group of predefined criteria, or of each of the questions (e.g., this candidate obtained 4 out of 5 for "Planification and organization").

---

3. For an overview of these results, consult the following meta-analyses: Conway, Jako and Goodman (1995); Huffcut and Arthur (1994); Marchese and Muchinsky (1993); McDaniel, Whetzel, Schmidt and Maurer (1994); Weisner and Cronshaw (1988); Wright, Lichtenfels and Pursell (1989); or the most recent narrative reviews: Campion, Palmer and Campion (1992); Harris (1989); Posthuma, Morgeson and Campion (2002).
4. See Dipboye (1992); Huffcutt and Arthur (1994).

Advantages in Relation to the Four Main Criteria

Structuring the selection interview improves its effectiveness in relation to these four criteria of success:

1. *Validity:* Research clearly demonstrates that the more an interview is structured, the greater the validity, so that structured interviews are clearly more effective than non-structured interviews in terms of accurately evaluating candidates.[5] It seems, however, that validity does not increase beyond a certain point.[6]

   Furthermore, an increasing number of studies indicate that there are significant differences in validity *between interviewers*; some interviewers are better than others and these are not necessarily the most experienced ones.[7] The structured interview seems to offer an advantage, since it minimizes these differences.[8]

2. *Reliability.* A substantial increase in the degree of reliability is a direct consequence of the standardized interview.[9] By neutralizing interviewers' inconsistencies immediately, at the time they are asking questions and evaluating responses, standardization produces evaluations that are by definition more reliable.

3. *Compliance with the law and the organization's policies, as well as legal defensibility.* A structured interview conforms better to the spirit of law and policy statements on the selection and promotion of personnel. Thus, when there is a dispute, it is much easier to successfully defend this kind of interview.[10] In addition, the structured interview makes it possible to limit the number of evaluation errors due to inconsistency[11] so there should be fewer disputes.

---

5. See the group of meta-analyses cited above.
6. Huffcutt and Arthur (1994).
7. See Campion *et al.* (1997).
8. See Dipboye (1992); Eder and Harris (1989); Posthuma *et al.* (2002).
9. See Eder and Harris (1999) and Posthuma (2002) as well as all the meta-analyses cited above.
10. Catano *et al.* (1997); Gatewood and Feild (2001); Taylor and O'Driscoll (1995); Terpstra, Mohamed and Kethley (1999).
11. Eder and Harris (1999); Posthuma *et al.* (2002).

4. *Candidates' reactions.* Candidates think that interviews which are conducive to uniform treatment are fairer.[12] On the other hand, a very structured interview, with no follow-up questions and no opportunity to touch on subjects other than those that were planned may in certain cases seem less fair, because it gives the candidates less opportunity to demonstrate their qualifications.[13] It is a fact, however, that the probability of a structured interview being contested is much lower than a traditional, less-structured interview, at least in the United States.[14]

Other Advantages

The structured interview has other advantages for interviewers, including the following:

1. *Processing the information.* With a structured interview, the information processing requirements for the interviewer are less demanding.[15] The interviewer can evaluate the candidates' responses more readily and decisions are made easier. This helps explain the increased validity and reliability of this kind of interview.
2. *Comparing candidates.* The uniform treatment of candidates makes it possible to compare them under the same conditions and in relation to the same requirements, and thus better evaluate the merits of each. All candidates are in the same situation and have the same opportunity to demonstrate their qualifications.
3. *Time management.* In the structured interview, the time allotted for each of the parties is determined on the basis of the information to be obtained. It is therefore easy to control the length of time it takes.

12. Catano *et al.* (1997).
13. Eder and Harris (1999).
14. Terpstra, Mohamed and Kethley (1999).
15. Posthuma *et al.* (2002).

Disadvantages

It must be noted that a very structured interview is like an oral examination, and its very nature reminds candidates that they are in an evaluation situation. Candidates want to show themselves in their best light and therefore may try to filter the information they provide. We will see later how to reduce the likelihood that the candidate will react in this way (see *Establish Facilitating Conditions* under *Step 4*).

THE JOB-RELATED INTERVIEW: CHARACTERISTICS AND ADVANTAGES

The best way to evaluate someone's success in a particular position would be to be able to observe the person doing the job.[16] Consequently, the more an interview for a position relates to the actual work to be done, the more it will make it possible to find the best candidate.[17] We will now return to the two main components of the interview and see how they can be related to the job.

a) **Interview questions** are job-related when they are developed to specifically measure the knowledge, skills or other personal characteristics identified during a job analysis as keys to performance.[18] The questions will be more job-related if they involve critical situations that actually occur in the workplace. For example, candidates could be asked a question about a management problem that recently occurred in the position they are applying for.

b) **Evaluation procedures** are job-related when the information obtained from the candidates is evaluated using a guide in which the expected responses come from a job analysis or are suggested by people who specialize in this job (*subject matter experts* or

16. Wernimont and Campbell (1968: cited in Dipboye, 1992).
17. In other words, a content-based validation approach should be followed (see Pettersen, 2000).
18. Catano *et al.* (1997).

SMEs). For example, before submitting the management problem to the candidates, a committee made up of the organization's best managers provides parts of the solution.

Advantages in Relation to the Four Main Criteria

The job-related interview can have the following advantages:

1. *Validity.* The more accurately the questions and the evaluation procedures reflect the job reality, the higher the validity of the interview.[19] Doing a job analysis or taking the advice of specialists (SMEs) are ways to achieve this.[20]

2. *Reliability.* On the other hand, focusing the interview on the job does not necessarily increase the reliability, except very slightly, to the extent that it contributes to limiting the content of the questions.[21]

3. *Compliance with the law and the organization's policies, as well as legal defensibility.* Conducting a job analysis is a basic condition of developing a valid instrument intended for personnel selection.[22] In addition, the spirit of the law and policies surrounding the selection and promotion of personnel require that all selection instruments be relevant to the job. In this way, when there is a dispute, it is much easier to defend an interview based on a job analysis, even more so if the questions and the expected responses reflect the job reality.[23]

4. *Candidates' reaction.* Job-related questions give the candidates a positive perception of the interview and the organization.[24] In fact, questions that are not job-related may be seen as inappropriate and lower the credibility of the selection process. They also

19. See Campion *et al.* (1997).
20. See Campion *et al.* (1997).
21. See Campion *et al.* (1997).
22. American Educational Research Association, American Psychological Association and National Council on Measurement in Education (1999).
23. See Catano *et al.* (1997); Gatewood and Feild (2001); Taylor and O'Driscoll (1995).
24. See Campion *et al.* (1997); Posthuma *et al.* (2002).

might affect the candidates' reactions, their interest in the organization and their intention of accepting the job or recommending the employer to other people.[25]

COMPARISON WITH OTHER EVALUATION METHODS

The structured job-related interview **compares favourably** with the best selection tools, as seen in Table 0.1.[26] In terms of **validity,** the structured interview is one of best tools. Most of the structured interviews examined in these studies are also job-related. Most of them included two types of job-related questions – situational and behavioural questions.[27] These questions are among the most effective and will be examined in *Step 3*. The structured interview also rates very well on two other criteria: **legality and defensibility,** and **candidates' reaction.**

Value added. The **costs** attached to the interview can be very high, particularly because of the preparation involved (especially if a scoring guide is developed), having to bring in the candidates, and the time the committee members must spend. Less expensive tools, like psychometric tests or written examinations, can be much more affordable to use. Still the **real question** remains – does the interview, in combination with less costly tools, increase the validity of the selection?[28]

---

25. See Eder and Harris (1999); Hausknecht, Day and Thomas (2004).
26. In this table, the values proposed for validity are based on a great number of studies. These indices are generic, however, and do not allow for a more precise distinction. For example, the validity estimate for general mental aptitude tests varies between 0.23 for non-specialized jobs and 0.58 for the very complex professional and managerial jobs (see Schmidt and Hunter, 1998). For the interview, validity can vary between 0.20 and 0.57 as the level of structure (standardization) increases (Huffcutt and Arthur, 1994). It should be noted, however, that in empirical studies of validity, the interviews considered non-structured were in fact sufficiently structured to create a quantitative analysis of the candidates, which means that the suggested validities in Table 0.1 are high compared to the validity of truly non-structured interviews (Dipboye, 1992). The other values in the table (legality and defensibility, candidates' reactions and costs) are approximate and cannot be considered reliable indices of reality with any rigour.
27. Eder and Harris (1999).
28. Dipboye (1992).

TABLE 0.1
Comparative analysis of various personnel selection methods

Selection method	Approximate criterion-related validity*	Legality and defensibility	Positive reaction from candidates	Cost
Work samples	0.54	Very high	Very high	Moderate to high
Mental aptitude tests	0.51	Low to moderate	Low	Low
Structured interviews	0.51	High to very high	High to very high	Moderate to high
Knowledge tests	0.48	Very high	Very high	Moderate
Non-structured interviews	0.38	Low to moderate	Variable	Low to moderate
Assessment centers	0.37	High to very high	High to very high	Very high
Personality inventories (conscientiousness)	0.31	Low to moderate	Low to moderate	Low
Interest inventories	0.10	Unknown	Moderate to high	Low

* Estimation of average validity proposed by Schmidt and Hunter (1998). In Pettersen (2000), p. 20.

According to these studies, it seems the answer is yes, at least in relation to psychometric tests measuring mental aptitudes. In fact, interviews make it possible to evaluate certain aspects that are not measured by these tests, so they help improve the overall validity of the selection process.[29] The benefits of interviews seem to be greater when they are structured, probably even more so when the questions are behavioural.[30]

Combining selection tools. Therefore, to maximize the validity of the overall selection process, it is very important to design an interview that will supplement and not duplicate the other selection tools, by evaluating aspects that the others do not.[31] For example, if validity

29. See Eder and Harris (1999); Gatewood and Feild (2001).
30. See Eder and Harris (1999); Huffcutt, Roth and McDaniel (1996); Posthuma *et al.* (2002).
31. Campion *et al.* (1997).

alone is considered, research indicates that to avoid redundancy between certain selection tools, the following combinations are probably the best.[32]

a) If **two tools** are to be used, consideration must be given to a general mental aptitude test to measure the candidate's potential, and a work sample or a structured interview to measure other aspects (e.g., an aptitude test to measure verbal comprehension, numerical reasoning and spatial perception, and an interview to assess job knowledge, oral communication and judgment).

b) If a **third tool** is added, a personality inventory is appropriate (e.g., to measure dedication or extroversion).

These recommendations are indirectly echoed in table 0.2. Later on, we will look at the other factors to be considered in choosing the interview as an evaluation method. (See *Choosing the Selection Criteria to Be Measured in the Interview* under *Step 2*.)

In spite of the above, it may be prudent to make use of two different tools to measure the same aspects (e.g., dedication may be measured by a personality inventory and an interview, or decision-making by a case study and an interview). This would enhance the information obtained.

TABLE 0.2
Approximate effectiveness of selection methods for various aspects measured*

Selection method	Aptitudes	Knowledge and skills	Personality and other personal qualities	Motivation
Aptitude tests	••••	–	–	–
Personality inventories	–	–	••••	••
Knowledge tests	•	••••	–	–
Work samples	•	••••	•	–
In-basket	•	••••	Unknown	–
Other simulations	•	••••	•	–
Interviews	••	••••	•••	•••

* Subjective evaluation ranging from not at all effective (–) to very effective (••••): Pettersen (2000), p. 22.

32. See Schmidt and Hunter (1998).

MOST COMMON OBJECTIONS TO USING THE STRUCTURED INTERVIEW

Despite the obvious relevance of the structured job-related interview, it is not the form of interview most commonly used by organizations. Some managers and other decision makers remain hesitant. We will examine the most common objections to the structured interview to evaluate how justifiable these objections are, and if necessary, determine how to correct for them.[33]

1. *Disproportion between the scale of the interview and the importance of the position to be filled.* As we will see in the following steps, preparing and conducting structured job-related interviews requires a great deal of time and effort. Efficiency-minded managers have legitimate concerns about whether the structured interview is a wise choice in all circumstances. For example, why invest time and money when *a)* the position to be filled is not an important one within the organization, *b)* the job is temporary or part-time, and *c)* a probation period allows the employment relationship to be freely terminated, so a selection mistake can be corrected?

   Before giving quick credence to these considerations, we should not underestimate the cost of a simplified selection process. First, a job that is done badly may have impacts far beyond the job itself. A misfiled file, a mechanical part incorrectly installed, incomplete follow-up or a client badly served can lead to problems with serious consequences. Second, the supervision of an incompetent employee usually requires a great deal of time, without any guarantee of success. Third, if employees are not able to do the job adequately, they will have to be dismissed and the selection process will have to begin all over again. Compared to this kind of scenario, the preparation and use of valid selection tools, particularly the structured interview, appear as a wise investment for the organization.[34]

33. See Eder and Harris (1999); Van Der Zee, Baker and Baker (2002).
34. Schmidt and Hunter (1998).

2. *Limited resources for preparing for and conducting interviews.* Many organizations do not have the human or financial resources to rigorously carry out all the steps required for structured interviews. In these circumstances, one might conclude that using a less restrictive approach is appropriate. However, this strategy, which responds to immediate constraints, is at risk of bearing a number of negative effects. In addition to leading to the problems described above, using a less structured interview provides lower validity and reliability levels, which increases the probability of hiring less qualified staff and lowering productivity.[35] Ultimately, short-term savings in hiring may be cancelled out in the medium term by costs and lost profits.[36]

3. *Influence of the interviewer's intuition and experience.* Some interviewers object that the structured interview, with its questions prepared in advance and based on the objective collection of information, leaves little room for intuition, a must for managers. Fortified by their broad experience in evaluation, they often think that they are intuitive enough to determine which applicant has the qualities required for the job. The structured interview seems somewhat superfluous to them.

   However, research tends to show that experience does not replace advantages of the structured interview.[37] The fact that decisions are made by an evaluation specialist does not necessarily guarantee their quality. Intuition has its place in the interview, though, in that it can suggest prompting or follow-up questions. Furthermore, if intuition persistently leads in the opposite direction from evaluations that are supposedly more objective, this may be the signal that more information needs to be collected, with another interview or by other evaluation methods. Finally, intuition is of absolutely no use with a candidate who must be given detailed feedback, or before a magistrate who must be convinced of the propriety of a selection process when there is a dispute.

35. Schmidt and Hunter (1998).
36. See the concept of utility in Pettersen (2000), chapter 1.
37. Campion *et al.* (1997).

4. *Preference for an informal process.* Some interviewers fear interviewees will have a negative reaction to structured interviews, undermining the organization's recruitment objectives from the outset. There are some grounds to that fear, but it has two important counterarguments. First of all, it must be remembered that a structured, job-related process has the advantage of being perceived by the applicants as a more equitable approach. Secondly, the structured interview does not impose a strict and forbidding atmosphere; quite the contrary. The emphasis on facilitating conditions and maintaining the candidate's self-confidence is an indication of this. (See *Step 4.*)
5. *Loss of control.* Having to ask the same questions of all candidates and use standardized evaluation tools may be seen by supervisors as a loss of control over their choice of staff. But if they are asked to participate in drawing up the questions and the evaluation tools, their concerns are reduced, because they will then be exercising some control over the selection process.
6. *Apparent absence of legal constraints.* Non-unionized organizations or those that do not have administrative boards to deal with complaints may not see the need for such a rigorous selection process. However, even if the legal aspect is less of a concern for them, lawsuits are still possible under legislation on discrimination or by appealing to the governing body of a professional organization. In addition to the structured interview's relatively low risk of litigation, we must remember that candidates generally react more favourably to it, which has positive consequences for the organization.

In summary, we can understand the hesitancy of some managers to invest time and money in structured interviews. However, the objections raised to justify less standardized interviews are not valid enough to make up for their disadvantages. Furthermore, it would be so much easier to get managers to better structure their interviews if senior administration formally recognized personnel selection as a high-priority task. The time has surely arrived to make managers and other decision makers responsible for the people they hire.

THE SELECTION INTERVIEW PROCESS

Preparing and conducting a structured job-related selection interview is a several-stage process. (See Figure 0.1.) Before conducting the interview, the job analysis must be carried out (*Step 1*), the selection criteria and the rules for making the decision must be determined (*Step 2*), and an interview guide containing the questions to be asked must be created (*Step 3*). Once the interview has been conducted (*Step 4*), the information obtained from the candidate must be evaluated (*Step 5*), and the hiring decision must be made (*Step 6*).

Each of these steps must be completely finished before moving on to the next one. For example, it is impossible to determine exact selection criteria prior to doing a job analysis, and this principle holds true for each of the other steps. In addition, the process can have no more value than its weakest step. A hastily put-together job analysis or an inappropriately conducted interview will definitely affect the quality of the evaluations and, ultimately, the hiring decision.

FIGURE 0.1
The selection interview process

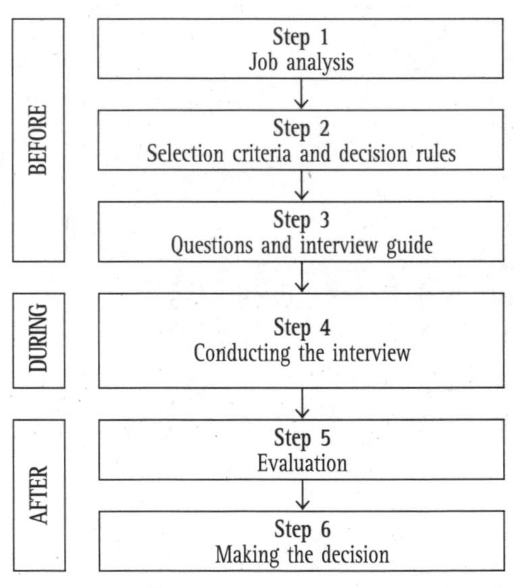

TABLE 0.3
The steps in the selection interview

Step 1 Job analysis	Understand the job and its context. The recommended steps are as follows: 1. Do a **job analysis**, which consists of gathering information about all essential aspects of a job, whether these are tasks, duties, or working conditions, in order to define and understand the job and its context as completely as possible. 2. Write the **job description for selection purposes**, a document summarizing all the information gathered from the job analysis. It is organized logically, chronologically or by topic.
Step 2 Selection criteria and decision rules	Define **which aspects must be evaluated** by interview and clarify the decision rules. The steps are as follows: 1. Turn the job aspects into **selection criteria** (the dimensions evaluated). 2. Choose the selection criteria to be **measured in the interview.** 3. Decide on the **indicators** or expected responses (information sought from the candidates). 4. Establish the **decision rules** by which the candidates will be selected at the end of the interview.
Step 3 Questions and interview guide	Prepare in detail the **way you will collect the required information** (indicators) from the candidates for the various selection criteria. You must: 1. Create **questions** that will obtain the information sought. 2. Organize the questions in a **sequence** that is logical for candidates and interviewers, and conducive to obtaining the information. 3. Prepare the **introduction** and **conclusion** for the interview. 4. Write the interview **guide.**
Step 4 Conducting the interview	Conduct the interviews, with the following guidelines in mind: 1. Remember the **objectives.** 2. Limit access to **ancillary information.** 3. Establish **facilitating conditions** with regard to the interview setting and the atmosphere, to help the candidate speak spontaneously. 4. Keep to the interview **structure** and stay in control so that you follow the guide. 5. Preserve the candidate's **self-esteem.** 6. Let the candidate speak; know how to **listen.** 7. Respect certain **rules of conduct.** 8. **Take notes** of your observations and the facts relevant to the evaluation criteria covered by the interview.
Step 5 Evaluation	Evaluate the information received from each candidate. You must: 1. Do the evaluation for each **question** or **criterion.** 2. If it is appropriate, use a **rating scale** whose descriptors are behavioural anchors or adjectives, but not comparisons. 3. Try to neutralize the **factors** that might distort the evaluation. 4. Use a committee made up of **several evaluators.** 5. Fill out an **evaluation form.**
Step 6 Making the decision	Decide on the individuals to be hired or who will move on to the next step in the selection process by assigning **overall scores** or setting multiple **cut-off scores.**

At each step, several tasks must be accomplished. (See Table 0.3). Methodically carrying out all these tasks may require considerable effort. You should remember that you need to strike a balance between the rigour and the effort deployed at each step and the hiring decision to be made and its consequences.

STEP 1

JOB ANALYSIS

A selection process must be based on an understanding of the job or group of jobs to be filled.[1] With a structured job-related interview, the questions and the evaluation guide must as far as possible be based on the real nature of the job to be filled. To achieve this, an analysis of the job and its context must be done.

1. Public Service Commission of Canada (2004).

There is a great deal of documentation available. Job analysis is a huge specialty and many books have been written about it.[2] We do not need to discuss all the knowledge and techniques in the field of job analysis here, but given its important role in preparing for and conducting an interview, a few elements bear review.

Definition. Job analysis is the process by which all the information about essential aspects of a job is gathered, including tasks, duties, responsibilities and working conditions.[3] This analysis makes it possible to determine what the person in this position does at work, how the work is done, with whom, for whom, why and in what context, as well as the resources at the incumbent's disposal. It has to take into account the scope and the level of the employee's responsibilities. In certain circumstances, future duties and functions of the job as well as its more immediate needs must be taken into consideration.[4]

Objective. In the selection context, a job analysis makes it possible to determine and understand all the aspects of a job or group of jobs in order to be able to define the selection criteria (the aspects to be evaluated in the candidates) in the following step. Therefore, you need a sound understanding of the tasks to be accomplished and the underlying rationale in order to understand the desired performance and the competencies and qualities required in the candidate.[5]

Job aspects to be analyzed. Table 1.1 presents the principle job aspects which can be analyzed. They do not all have to be analyzed to the same extent or in the same order as suggested here. The process needs to be adapted to the needs and constraints of the situation and the chosen approach.

---

2. See, among others, Brannick and Levine (2002); Gatewood and Feild (2001); Goldstein, Zedeck and Schneider (1993); Pettersen (2000); Schmitt and Chan (1998).
3. Pettersen (2000); Secrétariat du Conseil du trésor (2001).
4. Public Service Commission of Canada (2004).
5. Guion (1998).

TABLE 1.1
Aspects that can be part of the job analysis

1. **Job identification**
   - Job title, classification, etc.
   - Administrative unit
   - Immediate supervisor
2. **Summary of or rationale for the job**
   - The job's contribution to the organization's mission and the major responsibilities of the administrative unit
3. **What needs to be done**
   - Job elements
   - Tasks
   - Responsibilities (duties) or functions
4. **Expected outcomes**
   - Products or results*
   - Contributions of the job outputs to organizational mission and goals, implementation of programs, etc.
5. **Formal performance standards or performance evaluation criteria**
   - Qualitative and quantitative performance standards
6. **Job context**
   - Physical environment: space, temperature, cleanliness, noise, etc.
   - Working conditions: schedule, wages, contract, etc.
   - Administrative environment: mission, structure and process of coordination, level of responsibility, relationship to other jobs, etc.
   - Psychological and social environment: culture and climate
7. **Equipment and technology**
   - Equipment, tools, machinery, etc.
   - Specialized knowledge, technologies, techniques, etc.

* It may be that the products or results are already clearly indicated in "What must be done" or are implicit, in which case it is not necessary to clarify further.
Adapted from Pettersen (2000), p. 224.

The tasks to be carried out and the responsibilities to be assumed constitute "**what needs to be done.**" A *responsibility* or a *function* usually means a group of specific tasks. For example, the various tasks related to the budget (determining priorities, preparing the budget, controlling expenses) could constitute the "budget management" responsibility. A *task* is a group of job elements. The "budgetary control" task could include the following elements: approving expenses, recording the expenses under various budget items, etc.[6] The tasks and responsibilities do not all have the same importance: their frequency (or duration) and their scope must be specified. Enquiring about the main problems encountered and their implications is one way of assessing the importance of these aspects. If the candidates must successfully complete a **training program** that they have not yet taken, the activities and other elements of this program must be part of the analysis.[7]

Too often neglected in the job analysis, the **other aspects** presented in Table 1.1 must also be taken into consideration in order to draw a full picture of the ideal candidate. For example, the job context, particularly its administrative, psychological and social environment, will provide good indicators of the values and personality dimensions that will be required of the candidate.

Future needs. Future job needs, such as new technologies or long-term development programs, may also be taken into account. When it is clear that a job has a good chance of leading to a higher-level job, it may be appropriate to consider the tasks and responsibilities of this future job.[8]

Limiting the analysis to a subset. The analysis does not necessarily deal with all the tasks or job aspects. In certain circumstances, it could be limited to the aspects that are suited to the measurement instrument to be used. For example, a department head's job might include four areas of responsibility: *a*) strategic management, *b*) budgetary management, *c*) human resources management, and *d*) external communications. When designing the selection process, it could be decided that only candidates with accounting certification would be given an interview. Given this pre-selection criterion, it could also be decided not to

6. Pettersen (2000).
7. Society for Industrial and Organizational Psychology (2003).
8. Public Service Commission of Canada (2004); Society for Industrial and Organizational Psychology (2003).

evaluate certain aspects (e.g., budgetary management) in the interview. In this case, the job analysis for interview purposes could be limited to the three other areas of responsibility.

Methods and techniques for collecting information. To gather information on the various aspects of the job, several **methods** can be used. These include direct observation of people doing the job, individual interviews with these people or their supervisors, group interviews, questionnaires or keeping a journal. It might also be useful to consult existing job descriptions and other relevant documents (e.g., training manuals, the collective agreement). In short, any information that makes it possible to better understand the nature of the job to be done may be useful. Beyond these methods, various **techniques** are available, like the critical incident method (discussed later) and its variations, as well as many quantitative methods.[9]

With regard to job descriptions available from the human resources department or elsewhere, it should be noted that these documents are often designed to establish the organization's job classifications, not for determining required competences and others selection criteria. In addition, these job descriptions do not necessarily provide essential information, such as the way the job must be carried out, the expected outcomes or other organizational aspects like the company's culture. These aspects can however influence the type and level of skills required, or other necessary personal qualities.[10] In this regard, the incumbent or the immediate supervisor can represent a good source of information.

In practice, the investment needed for a job analysis will vary according to the circumstances. An important position, or a job occupied by a large number of people, may justify a more comprehensive analysis.

---

9. See Pettersen (2000).
10. Public Service Commission of Canada (2004).

WRITING A JOB DESCRIPTION FOR SELECTION PURPOSES

Definition. When the job analysis is complete, it is convenient to gather all the information obtained in one document. This document constitutes the job description for selection purposes. The information presented can be structured in relation to the various aspects outlined in Table 1.1. Under "**what needs to be done**" (i.e., the tasks to be accomplished and the responsibilities to be assumed as part of the job), the information should be presented according to a logical structure, which for the most part is chronological or topical. Appendix A presents an example of a job description for selection purposes. The tasks, organized by topics, are grouped according to the main responsibilities of the job.

The job description written for selection purposes may be different from the existing job description (e.g., the one from human resources or the collective agreement), since that one is generally used to classify jobs or organize the work. The job description for selection purposes must be more detailed and provide information not included in existing job descriptions, such as expected results or the administrative or psychological environment.

The job description and the validity of the interview. Although it is recommended, writing a job description is not a strict prerequisite for validating the selection process. If the job analysis is done meticulously, it is possible to define and understand the aspects of a job adequately and to determine the selection criteria, without necessarily writing up a job description. Nevertheless, it is almost essential to take note of the information gathered, particularly if there is a lot of it, or if the interview or any other part of the selection process may have to be justified.

Verification. It must be ensured that the information has been understood, set out and organized accurately by the person or persons doing the job analysis. This verification is usually done by submitting the job description to incumbents of that same position, or immediate supervisors, or another expert in the field, called a *subject matter expert* or SME.

Report on the approach followed. A detailed report on the approach followed may be very useful in case of a litigation. In addition to the job description, the report could include the following sections: *a*) a description of the techniques used to collect the information, *b*) the documents analyzed (e.g., the description of existing tasks, training manuals), *c*) the names of incumbents and other people who provided information, with their titles, their level in the organizational structure, and their qualifications, and *d*) the qualifications of the people who did the job analysis.

The quality of the job analysis process may be determinative in demonstrating the validity of the selection interview. In this regard, the methods and techniques for collecting information should be systematic and objective, be well documented, and provide information that is current and representative of the job.[11]

THE CRITICAL INCIDENT METHOD

Of all the various job analysis methods that may be used to prepare a job-related interview, the most commonly used is the critical incident method, or one of its derivatives.[12] Moreover, this method is practically indispensable to the development of situational questions, which often play a primary role in the structured interview.[13]

Description. Initially proposed by Flanagan (1954), the critical incident method consists of asking experts (i.e., incumbents of the job in question, immediate supervisors or anyone else who has sufficient knowledge of the job) to provide examples of actual situations in which people doing the job were particularly **effective** or particularly **ineffective**. The expert may be the person who was in the situation, or another person doing the same job, or an observer in any capacity. The goal is to obtain a description of specific behaviours and their

11. Pettersen (2000).
12. Campion *et al.* (1997).
13. Taylor and O'Driscoll (1995).

Example of a positive incident (effective behaviour)

Context	The company had once produced a line of garden lighting products and the operation was a complete fiasco. However, when the company hired me as production manager, I was already thinking that the market for garden lighting was going to grow and it could be a major product line for the company. So I wanted to design new products in collaboration with the designer and then launch this new line. Of course, some members of the team had doubts. I needed to convince them. They knew me a little, and they said, "We already did that and it was a mistake. If we do this, we'll just be starting all over again." I had to consolidate the team and prove that together we could succeed.
Behaviour	First of all, I did a quick market research study. I looked at stores specializing in landscaping and I noticed that the designers were now taking exterior lighting into account when they were drawing up plans. I also did a small survey with our distributors. In almost every case, they told me that several of their clients were disappointed with the choices available to them in exterior lighting. So then I worked with two of my technicians and we produced a few sketches. With all this information in hand, I met with the marketing director and presented my ideas. He was really excited. Together we drew up a proposal for the board and added an estimate of production costs and potential benefits to deal with the probable questions from the accounting department.
Result	Everybody's first reaction was, "That won't work!" I made note of all their objections and then I responded to every one of them using the documentation in my proposal. The marketing director only intervened at the end with his approval. The Board gave the go-ahead to a pilot project, which was a great success. Now the company has a full range of exterior lighting products.

Example of a negative incident (ineffective behaviour)

Context	An employee (the incumbent) was approached by a colleague who asked him to help him retrieve a lost file, a task that was not part of his regular duties.
Behaviour	He told his colleague, "You should have kept a backup copy. It's not my responsibility to find other people's lost files."
Result	The colleague was not able to finish his report on time. He never again asked this employee for help.

Source: Taylor and O'Driscoll (1995, p. 22).

consequences, as they have been observed, and not general opinions, explanations or judgments of these events.[14] In this regard, it is important to include job incumbents and supervisors among the experts.

The descriptions of these situations, called *critical incidents*, must be taken from real events and relate to a specific situation. They must present the **context** in which the person was acting, the person's **behaviour** and the **outcomes** that resulted from that behaviour.

Methods of collecting critical incidents. Job experts may recount these incidents in various ways: by questionnaire, in small group discussions, or in individual interviews. Questionnaires have the advantage of being economical, but they do not permit the interviewer to clarify an ambiguous or incomplete incident. When the number of experts is large, a few group meetings are preferable to many individual ones.

Preparation. No matter what methods are to be used, careful preparations must be made, and an appropriate questionnaire or interview guide drawn up. Appendix B presents examples of tools for collecting critical incidents. The questionnaire is based on Flanagan (1954) and the interview guide is a variation proposed by Spenser and Spenser

---

14. See the summary in Gatewood and Feild (2001); Taylor and O'Driscoll (1995).

(1993). If the incidents are reported at meetings, it is preferable to ask each of the experts to write down a certain number of positive and negative incidents before the meeting.

Overall tasks or only certain aspects. The incidents described by the experts may deal with the job's tasks overall, or specific tasks (e.g., budgetary management, dealing with customer complaints) or specific dimensions (e.g., leadership, sense of responsibility). When the job analysis and description has already been done and the critical incident method is used to prepare interview questions, the experts could be asked to suggest incidents that deal with the selection criteria that will be measured by the interview.

Analysis of the critical incidents. Once the critical incidents have been gathered, they can be grouped in various ways: according to the job responsibilities or functions, or by selection criteria (see *Step 2*), etc. Usually it is more useful to organize them by selection criteria, especially if they must be used to draw up situational questions used in the evaluation interview (see *Step 3, Situational Questions*). Three or four different incidents must be obtained for each category.

THE COMPETENCY-BASED APPROACH

In recent years, a so-called "competency-based" approach has appeared. It is used in almost every area of human resource management,[15] including personnel selection.[16] Some believe that the competency-based approach is based on a job analysis that is different from the "classic" approach described above. Others see the distinction between these two approaches as more subtle than that.[17]

---

15. Berge *et al.* (2002); Dingle and Williams (1999); Dubnicki and Williams (1990); Hoffman (1999); Lasnier (2000); Lawler III, Ledford Jr. and Chang (1993); May (1999); Milkovich and Newman (1999).
16. Dubnicki and Williams (1990); Durivage (2004); Farnham and Stevens (2000); Rowe (1995); Slivinski and Miles (1996); Spencer and Spencer (1992).
17. See Shippmann *et al.* (2000).

Without wanting to settle this debate, the competency-based approach can be said to distinguish itself in two ways. First of all, rather than dissect a job into its specific tasks, the competency-based approach instead stresses the job's main responsibilities, often analyzing several jobs at once, with the aim of determining the competencies that are common to a group of jobs (e.g., a sector of an organization, a hierarchical level). Secondly, the competency-based approach pays particular attention to the link between the competencies required for each job and the organization's strategic direction: an overall understanding of the organization, its mission, strategy, stage of development, culture and values and its environment.[18] The competency-based approach is also marked by its weaknesses, which make it less rigorous, at least up to now, than the more traditional job analysis.[19]

The competency-based approach is therefore more generic and holistic in nature, which lends itself to a group of similar jobs, like administrative support or sales positions. Later on we will discuss how this approach has certain consequences, especially on the way selection criteria and interview questions are drawn up.

18. Durivage (2004), Shippmann *et al.* (2000); Slivinski and Miles (1997); Tovey (1994).
19. Shippmann *et al.* (2000).

STEP 2

SELECTION CRITERIA AND DECISION RULES

The job analysis has led us to understand and define the various aspects of the job and its context. *Step 2* consists of determining the knowledge, skills and other characteristics that make a candidate suitable for the job. These required qualities have several names: requirement profile, competency profile, worker or job specifications, or statement of qualities. They are also called predictors or dimensions evaluated. In the present work, they are designated as **selection criteria.**

As seen in Table 0.1, this step has four stages. First, the job has to be turned into selection criteria. Second, from among these criteria, the ones to be evaluated in the selection interview must be chosen. Third, indicators must be established. These indicators, which are observable during the interview, will be used to measure to what extent the candidate responds to each of the criteria. Fourth, it is a good idea to plan which rules will take precedence in evaluating the candidates and making the decision.

TURNING THE JOB INTO SELECTION CRITERIA

Suggested approach. Turning the job and its context into selection criteria is done in three phases:

- Phase 1: **Choose** the aspects of the job to be evaluated;
- Phase 2: **Identify the requirements** needed to accomplish these job aspects: the selection criteria;
- Phase 3: **Determine the relative value** of each of the selection criteria.[1]

In **phase** 1, remember that it is possible to limit yourself to a single part of the job. To select a teacher, for example, you could decide to focus the interview only on classroom responsibilities and the interest in teaching, and evaluate the other aspects of the job by other means.

Phase 2 can be done in two different ways. The first is direct and makes no inferences. The job components need to be grouped according to similarity. For a secretary's position, for example, if a particular software must be used to write documents in both English and French, the criteria are *a*) writing documents in English, *b*) writing documents in French, and *c*) use of the software. In the case of the job analysis for the position of city manager, you could group the main tasks into six responsibilities: *a*) budgetary management, *b*) regulatory management, *c*) complaints and claims management, *d*) program and project management, *e*) internal management and personnel supervision, and *f*) external communications management. Each responsibility therefore becomes a selection criterion, which is defined directly by the tasks included in this responsibility.

1. This section is largely based on Pettersen (2000).

The second approach is indirect and is carried out by inferring the **underlying requirements.** It consists of determining the knowledge, skills and other personal characteristics that a person must possess to accomplish each task or activity involved in the job. For the city manager's job, for instance, it could be determined that budgetary management requires *a*) accounting knowledge, *b*) analytical skills, and *c*) attention to detail. Regulatory management demands *a*) knowledge of law, *b*) the ability to understand legal texts, *c*) analytical abilities, and *d*) judgment; and so on for all the other responsibilities. It should be noted that the work environment and the specific context of the job also must be taken into consideration when determining requirements. For example, if the city regulations change frequently, it would be desirable to add the criterion "Adaptability and openness to change" to the list of personal characteristics. The requirements thus identified are then grouped according to their similarities to form selection criteria. In this example, the selection criteria could be *a*) knowledge in accounting and law, *b*) understanding of legal authorities, *c*) analytical skills, *d*) judgment, *e*) attention to detail, etc. It should be noted that the two approaches can be combined for the same job, i.e., some job components can be dealt with using inference and others without.

Inferring the underlying requirements of each task in a job requires time and effort. In addition to analyzing each task, the many requirements that result must be grouped to form selection criteria. As well, each time a task is modified, which happens frequently these days, the selection criteria should be reviewed. Given these drawbacks, many professionals prefer to infer requirements only for the larger job responsibilities or groups of tasks. It seems that this certainly less burdensome way of doing things makes it possible to identify the same selection criteria as though analyzing each of the tasks. An example of this approach, i.e., by inference for large groups of tasks, can be found in Appendix C.

Phase 3 concerns the weighting of the selection criteria. The value for each criterion must be based on the importance of the associated tasks or responsibilities. Two aspects should be linked to the value: the time devoted to these tasks and responsibilities, and their consequences.[2] Weighting of the criteria will be discussed in *Step 6.*[3]

Existing lists of selection criteria. Whichever approach is adopted, it is important not to reinvent the wheel. Take inspiration from existing lists of selection criteria, even if you have to revise the definitions, adding or subtracting criteria according to the job specifics. A list of selection criteria for management positions is presented in Appendix D. It can be used as a starting point, which will save time and effort. Many other selection criteria lists exist which have been carefully drawn up according to rigorous methodologies.[4]

KSAO Typology. Selection criteria belong to different categories. The most widely used typology in North America has four categories: *job knowledge* (*K*), *skills* (*S*), *abilities* (*A*) and *other characteristics* (*O*). This important typology, known by its initials, KSAO, is detailed in Table 2.1. In KSAO typology, as in most of the lists suggested in the specialized books, training and experience are not mentioned as selection criteria because these aspects are in fact indicators. This will be dealt with later in *Determining Indicators or Expected Responses.*

Work behaviour components. The components of the KSAO model can be structured so as to provide an account of an individual's work performance. Figure 2.1 presents a schematic diagram that is useful in this regard.[5] We note first of all that the KSAOs can be used to define three large elements that influence work behaviour: ability, willingness and personality. **Ability**, or what a person is capable of doing, depends

2. Pettersen (2000); Secrétariat du Conseil du trésor (2001).
3. Most of the approaches suggested in specialized works use the same phases, sometimes with a few extra explanations (e.g., the limits for a given job of defining criteria without inference, and in too specialized a manner) or additional ways of ensuring validity of the selection criteria established (e.g., methodologies for determining the relative value of the criteria). See Gatewood and Feild (2001); Pettersen (2000).
4. Some of these lists are presented in summary in Pettersen (2000, p. 243). See also the remarkable work of Slinvinski and Miles (1997) and Tett, Guterman, Bleier, and Murphy (2000).
5. Adapted from Pettersen and Jacob (1992).

TABLE 2.1
KSAO selection criteria categories

	Type of characteristic	Definition	Examples
K	Job knowledge	All the information on facts, rules or procedures directly related to carrying out an activity, task or function. Knowledge is the basis for cognitive skills.	Knowing how to spell, use software, understanding employee preferences, the organization's strategic plan, the collective agreement, etc.
S	Skills	Observable performance (competence) in carrying out a learned physical or motor activity or task (i.e., muscular movements, sight)	Applying the brakes, putting holes in metal, keyboarding, inserting letters in envelopes, etc.
	Cognitive skills (*skills* or *abilities*, depending on the author)	Observable performance (competence) in carrying out an activity, a learned task or a cognitive function.	Preparing the department budget, using a computer to create financial statements, questioning a client to establish the client's needs, developing a complaint classification system, etc.
A	Cognitive and psychomotor abilities (*abilities* or *aptitudes*, depending on the author)	Potential abilities that influence the learning and execution of an activity, task or function. General abilities that the person has before learning a particular task.	Verbal aptitude, ability to learn, spatial perception, eye-hand coordination, etc. Ability to understand written instruction, make oral presentations, do basic calculations, describe a situation, write sentences, etc.
O	Other characteristics	Personality traits, needs, values, etc.	Introversion, emotional stability, need for respect, honesty, etc.

Source: Pettersen (2000), p. 242.

on his or her aptitudes and competencies, which are composed of the knowledge (K), and skills (S) that a person has acquired through training and experience. **Willingness** is what a person is willing to do, or what we could call motivation. Needs, values, attitudes and interests are the variables at the root of the motives and goals that cause individuals to act, and these motives and goals are the source of their

FIGURE 2.1
Components of work behaviour

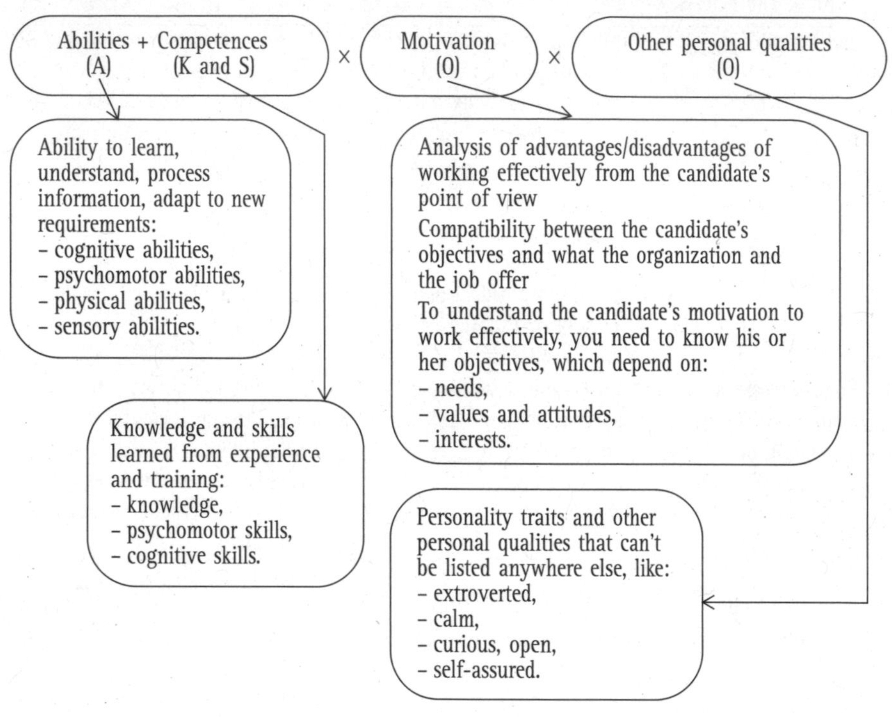

motivation. **Personality** traits and other personal qualities colour the individual's ways of being and acting. Motivation and personality variables are listed indiscriminately under O in the KSAO model.

DEFINING THE SELECTION CRITERIA

There is no ideal list of all selection criteria. The many lists that are available may be equally worthwhile as long as they comply with a few basic rules.

Rule 1 – Relevance. Each selection criterion must deal with a significant aspect of the job. To ensure this, it may be useful to *a)* make a two-way table establishing the relationship between each criterion and the corresponding job components, or *b)* use job experts to make a decision on the relevance of each criterion selected.[6]

Rule 2 – Stability. The selection criteria should be restricted to the knowledge, skills and other characteristics that a person must have before being hired, and eliminate the elements that a person can learn with a brief period of familiarization with the job.[7] As much as possible, the criteria should target the candidate's stable characteristics, the ones that change very little over time.[8]

Rule 3 – Generalizability. Similarly, it is not reasonable to require a competence that can only be acquired after hiring, or that only candidates who have already held the position or received training specific to the job can have. For example, it would seem obviously inappropriate for an interview question to deal with specific knowledge about the mechanics of a department's administration.[9]

Rule 4 – Completeness. The selection criteria as a whole must cover all the important components of the job under consideration, or a subset of these components, if appropriate. It should be noted that a complete profile, depending on the complexity of the job and the extent of the criteria, might contain 6 to 15 selection criteria (up to a maximum of 20). Figure 2.1 summarizes the broad categories of criteria for predicting job performance. All categories should be present in a complete profile of requirements.

Rule 5 – Clarity. Each selection criterion must have a clear and unequivocal definition on the basis on which a behaviour or any other indicator can be reliably classified.[10]

---

6. Dipboye (1992); Gatewood and Feild (2001); Pettersen (2000).
7. Society for Industrial and Organizational Psychology (2003); Taylor and O'Driscoll (1995).
8. Gatewood and Feild (2001); Pettersen (2000).
9. Pettersen (2000); Public Service Commission of Canada (2004).
10. Byham (1987).

Examples

a) *Leadership*: ability to direct and influence the way a person or a group of people carry out activities so that established objectives are achieved.*

b) *Leadership*: ability to use appropriate methods to guide individuals (subordinates, colleagues, superiors) or groups in accomplishing tasks.**

* Unless otherwise noted, all the examples of selection criteria descriptions come from various organizations and are reproduced in full.

** Adapted from Byham (1987), under "Index de questions préparées," p. 49.

The first definition of leadership, although it appears valid, does not specify the nature of the methods that the leader might implement in order to influence others. So a manager who used threats or blackmail would show leadership according to this definition. This would probably not be the case with the second definition, which is more explicit, mentioning that the methods must be appropriate. It is not easy to write unambiguous definitions, which is why it is important to use existing lists that have been carefully written.

Rule 6 – Independence. As in all typologies, the selection criteria must be mutually exclusive, or independent. Two criteria are independent when the evaluation a candidate receives for one of the criteria is not linked to the evaluation obtained for the other one.

Examples

a) *Written expression*: Able to communicate thoughts in writing clearly and precisely.

b) *Oral expression*: Able to clearly and precisely communicate thoughts orally.

In these examples, the two criteria are independent because it is very possible for a candidate to be competent orally without being able to write well, and vice versa. There is no absolute link between these two competences.

Examples

a) *Mobilization*: Able to get his or her team to rally around a project, subscribe to the organization's vision, values and objectives, and work together to produce the expected results.

b) *Supervision and control:* Able to get his or her team to achieve the established objectives, evaluate the performance obtained, measure the difference between objectives and results, and make the appropriate corrections.

This time there is a problem of redundancy between the two criteria. The ability to get the team to achieve established objectives (under *Supervision and control*) clearly encroaches on the *Mobilization* criterion. The way this is written causes two problems. The redundant part of the criterion is not useful, since it is already included in the other criterion. It is also confusing, because the same behaviour or indicator can be simultaneously classified under two criteria.

When two criteria are not independent, there are two possible **solutions.** The **first** is to go over the definitions to try and eliminate the redundancy. It would be easy, for example, to remove "able to get the team to achieve established objectives" from *Supervision and control* and thereby correct the situation. The **second** solution is to make one single criterion out of the two overlapping ones. This solution is not appropriate in the above example. However if *Leadership* and *Mobilization* were both wanted in relation to the same job, they could be joined to become *Leadership and mobilization.*

In practice, criteria are rarely completely independent from each other, people being as complex as they are. For example, having good interpersonal skills usually facilitates leadership, the ability to establish a contact network and work as part of a team. Consequently the independence of criteria should not be viewed as an absolute, but rather an objective to be achieved as closely as possible.

Rule 7 – Homogeneity. Each selection criterion must be homogenous, so that its various components belong to the same concept. Otherwise, these components form different criteria (this is the reciprocal of Rule 6). Two components are homogenous when the evaluation obtained by a candidate for one of these components is necessarily linked to the evaluation received for the other.

Example

- *Planning and organization*: Able to establish schedules and stages of development and distribute the work and the responsibilities in a balanced manner while maintaining an appropriate atmosphere of communication within the team.

It is clear that this criterion includes at least two distinct components: *a*) planning (establish schedules and stages of development) and organization (distribute the work and the responsibilities in a balanced manner) and *b*) maintaining an appropriate atmosphere of communication. In such a case, the criterion must be broken down into its non-homogenous parts; in this example, we would have Planning and organization and Managing a team atmosphere.

Following are two other examples of ambiguous selection criteria established by a large organization. In addition to problems with their definition, these criteria present more than one component. Can you identify the components found in these criteria?

Examples

- *Interpersonal communication*: Is eloquent, and flexible enough to adapt to different clients, is able to listen and understand the message (both verbal and non-verbal), to share in-depth thoughts and to adapt to other people's reactions and to diverse views.
- *Decision-making*: Deals with a problem as a whole in order to determine causes and possible solutions. Makes decisions, even in difficult situations.

CHOOSING THE SELECTION CRITERIA TO BE MEASURED BY INTERVIEW

Suggested approach. Once the selection criteria have been defined, it is time to choose those that will be evaluated by interview. Several selection tools can be used to evaluate all the criteria with the candidates: résumé analysis, job knowledge tests, simulations, or references. Each tool will allow you to measure one or more criteria, and the same criterion may be evaluated by more than one tool. The term "selection tool" is synonymous with evaluation method, selection method, measuring instrument. Before establishing the criteria that will be measured by the interview, **it is important to consider:**

1. *The relative effectiveness of the selection tools.* Not all tools are equally effective for all the criteria to be measured. Psychometric tests, for example, are unsurpassed in their ability to measure mental aptitudes, whereas pencil and paper tests measure knowledge adequately.[11] Refer to Table 0.1, *Comparative analysis of various personnel selection methods.*

2. *The most effective selection criteria for the interview.* The interview can measure several types of criteria, depending on the questions asked. Due to its **interpersonal** nature, the interview is very useful for evaluating criteria such as:
   - interpersonal and social skills;
   - teamwork;
   - leadership;
   - motivation for the available job (a fit between the candidate's values, objectives, interests and attitudes and the organization's culture, atmosphere, objectives and standards); and
   - decision-making.[12]

11. Gatewood and Feild (2001); Taylor and O'Driscoll (1995).
12. Catano *et al.* (1997); Campion *et al.* (1997); Eder and Harris (1999); Gatewood and Feild (2001); Posthuma *et al.* (2002).

Although this may be more difficult, the interview could also be used to evaluate **personality** traits such as:

- initiative;
- sense of responsibility and reliability;
- perseverance; and
- flexibility.[13]

Finally, the interview certainly has the ability to measure **knowledge**. However, if there are many questions, and the expected responses are relatively specific, it would be better to choose another method, such as a test, and reserve the interview for the criteria that are more difficult to measure with other tools. As we have seen, the interview should complement rather than duplicate the other evaluation methods.[14]

3. *The interview's inability to measure a large number of criteria at once.* Specialists, backed by the research, agree that the interview should be confined to a small number of criteria, without specifying exactly how many.[15] Trying to use a large number of criteria often results in superficial evaluations that do not have a great deal of value. Given the usual 60 to 90 minutes available for an interview, it seems reasonable to limit the number of criteria (from three to seven, approximately). You should also think about the number of questions to ask per criterion, and the complexity of the questions, since candidates can take five to ten minutes to answer a moderately complex question like a situational or behavioural question of the type that will be introduced in the next section.

13. Catano *et al.* (1997); Eder and Harris (1999); Gatewood and Feild (2001).
14. Campion *et al.* (1997).
15. Byham (1987); Gatewood and Feild (2001).

DETERMINING THE INDICATORS OR EXPECTED RESPONSES

Suppose that *leadership* is chosen as a selection criterion and defined as follows:

> *Leadership*: the ability to use appropriate methods to manage the activities of a person or a group in order to achieve established objectives.

According to this definition, how do you evaluate in an interview whether a candidate has leadership? How do you recognize whether the person has this quality?

Definition of an indicator. It is not enough to define the selection criteria according to the appropriate rules as outlined above (See *Turning the Job into Selection Criteria*). They also have to be made observable. To do so, you must determine the observable manifestations and the tangible signs that make it possible to evaluate as objectively as possible, during the interview, to what extent the candidate fulfills this criterion. These manifestations or signs are called indicators. The indicators correspond to the expected responses to the interview questions or information sought from the candidate. It is important to choose objective indicators that reduce the interviewers' subjectivity to a minimum during evaluation. (e.g., the indicator "shows initiative" calls for subjectivity). The following are examples of indicators for evaluating leadership:[16]

Examples

- Gets a person or a group of people to subscribe to an idea or a way of proceeding
- Influences the position of those in authority in order to obtain desired results
- Becomes accepted and takes leadership of the group
- Motivates personnel effectively to achieve desired objectives

---

16. Adapted from the *Recueil d'indicateurs de comportements recherchés en emploi pour l'évaluation du personnel de la fonction publique québécoise*, produced by the Office des ressources humaines and reproduced in the appendix to Module 3 – *Moyens d'évaluation écrits, pratiques et oraux*.

The role of indicators. It is neither realistic nor necessary to establish all possible indicators for a selection criterion, for the simple reason that there are an unlimited number: the same criterion can be manifested in any number of ways. A representative **sample** is enough. Indicators actually play three roles:

a) They **define** the criterion in concrete terms. For instance, the examples of leadership indicators explain what leadership is.

b) They guide the preparation of **questions** that will be asked during the interview.

c) They allow **evaluation** of the candidate on this criterion by providing observable, even quantifiable, manifestations. If, for a given criterion, you are unable to determine observable indicators during an interview, then it is impossible to evaluate this criterion using this tool. Thus you realize in advance that it is sometimes difficult to evaluate certain criteria in an interview (e.g., honesty, reliability, punctuality, etc.).

Before, during or after preparing the questions. The indicators can be established before, during or after preparing the interview questions, depending on the interviewer's way of working and the kind of questions planned. However, it is critical that the questions enable the interviewer to observe the chosen indicators and obtain the information sought from the candidates.

Indicator categories. There are several categories of indicators, and a type of interview question that corresponds to each category. These categories are presented in Table 2.2. Reading over the table, one can see that the examples of indicators for evaluating leadership mentioned previously all belong to one category, which is that of behaviour directly observable in the work situation. This is valid, provided that the interview is made up of appropriate questions for this category of indicators. (This aspect will be dealt with at the same time as the various types of questions are presented in *Step 3*.)

Training and experience as indicator categories. Training and experience are not in themselves competencies sought in the candidate, in the sense that they are not knowledge, skills, aptitudes, or personal

Table 2.2
Indicator categories

Criterion evaluated: *Leadership*

a) **Behaviours and results that may be observed in the interview**
Examples of indicators
- Takes the initiative during the interview (e.g., strikes up a conversation when first entering the room).
- Presents a clear and articulate vision of what he or she wants to do.
- Gains the attention, respect and confidence of the committee members.

b) **Behaviours and results that may be observed in the work situation (or taken from the candidate's past history) and expressed verbally in the interview**
Examples of indicators
- Gains the attention, respect and confidence of others.
- Is able to get a person or a group to adopt an idea or a way of going about things.
- Influences the positions of those in authority in order to obtain the desired results.
- Becomes accepted and takes leadership of the group.

c) **Behavioural intentions expressed verbally in the interview**
Examples of indicators
- Put in a hypothetical situation, says that he or she would consult employees.
- Says that he or she would accept and seek responsibility.

d) **Professional and technical knowledge**
Examples of indicators
- Mentions the parameters to which his or her management style must be adapted.
- Suggests ways of motivating employees.

e) **Interests, motivations, aspirations, goals, opinions or attitudes expressed verbally in the interview**
Examples of indicators
- Says he or she likes supervision.
- Says he or she wants to have more responsibility.
- Says he or she believes in accountability as a way of involving people.

f) **Training and experience**
Examples of indicators
- Bachelor degree in management.
- Practical training in supervision.
- Reading biographies of great leaders.
- Number of years of relevant experience.
- Reporting level.
- Has led a team of employees.
- Specific accomplishments, honours, awards.

characteristics. We should rather consider them as indications that the candidate *probably* possesses this knowledge, and these skills, aptitudes and personal characteristics *at a certain level.* Nevertheless, they remain quite accurate indications, and not costly, so they can be used as selection criteria, as long as we remember two things. **First**, a degree or some years of experience do not guarantee competence. To know the exact level of a person's knowledge, skills and aptitudes, we have to go to other, much more reliable indicators, such as the candidate's answers to questions designed to measure these aspects directly. **Second**, a person may very well have some of the competencies sought, without having the appropriate degree or required experience.

Rules for Determining Indicators

There are three rules for determining indicators.

Rule 1 – Representativeness. The sample of chosen indicators must represent all the aspects of the corresponding selection criterion.

Rule 2 – Relevance and absence of bias. Each indicator must be relevant and clearly linked to the corresponding selection criterion. Indicators that are biased or have cultural implications should be avoided: for example, maintaining visual contact is not a socially acceptable behaviour in certain cultures.

Rule 3 – Observable in the interview situation. Each indicator must be observable in response to the questions that will be asked during the interview.

An example of definition of a selection criterion (interpersonal relationships) and its indicators is shown in Table 2.3.

ESTABLISHING DECISION RULES

Decision rules must be set in order to provide a framework for the process of evaluating the candidates and making decisions about them at the end of the interview (and after other selection tools, if need be). It is essential, for the objectivity of the process and its appearance of

TABLE 2.3
Example of a selection criterion definition and its indicators

Criterion evaluated: *Interpersonal relations*
Definition - Maintains friendly and pleasant relationships with others. - Does not act in a way that makes others tense or uncomfortable. - Tries to understand the needs and feelings of the people he or she is talking to.
Indicators that this person possesses the criterion: - Does not interrupt the person he or she is talking to unnecessarily. - Restates the person's remarks. - Does not try to impose his or her point of view excessively. - Smiles. - Speaks of others in positive or respectful terms. - Speaks of others perceptively, considering their points of view, motivations, limits, etc. - Takes measures to understand others' needs and feelings. - When there are differences, looks for solutions that respect others' self-esteem and dignity. - Experience working with the public, in a helping relationship, as a team, etc. - Has training in interpersonal relations.

Adapted from Pettersen (2000), p. 284.

objectivity, that these rules be set from the very beginning, before knowing the candidates and what their results are. These rules deal, among other things, with how the criteria and the selection tools should be weighted, the eliminatory nature of certain criteria or selection tools, and the use of an overall result or a sequential decision-making process, etc. These aspects will be dealt with in *Step 6*.

STEP 3

THE INTERVIEW GUIDE

Having defined the selection criteria in the previous step, we will now discuss in detail **how to collect information** from the candidates in relation to the various selection criteria. To do so, we need to prepare the questions that will be asked at the interview and a guide for the interview procedure. (See Table 0.3, *The steps in the selection interview.*) This step requires several operations and some knowledge.

STANDARDIZING THE QUESTIONS AND THEIR SEQUENCE

There are four levels of standardization or structure in interview questions and their sequencing:[1]

1. Campion *et al.* (1997); Huffcutt and Arthur (1994).

Level 1 No structure – no formal plan, no prepared questions.

Level 2 Low structure – list of topics to cover.

Level 3 High structure – list of initial questions that the interviewer can adapt to each candidate, with the possibility of prompting or follow-up questions.

Level 4 Maximum structure – exactly the same questions put to all the candidates, in the same way and order and without prompting or follow-up questions.

The ideal structure for questions should fall at about Level 3 or slightly below Level 4. There are several reasons for this. As mentioned earlier, the more structured the interview, the higher the validity. However, there does not seem to be any significant increase in validity beyond the third level of structure.[2] In addition, despite a higher degree of reliability and objectivity, maximum standardization of the process has several disadvantages (see *The Structured Interview, Advantages and Disadvantages*). Therefore, it may be beneficial not to have maximum structure in some situations. First of all, interviewers often have important questions that only apply to one candidate. Second, many interviewers think that it is excessive to plan all the questions and not be able to ask prompting or follow-up questions. Third, some interviewers ask additional questions on particular points, even if attempts are made to interrupt them. However, in a situation where there may be a lawsuit, a less-structured interview is more difficult to defend, and therefore more risky.[3]

Even though interviewers are fully justified in using the maximum level of structure, they must however remember that they have an obligation to help candidates, if necessary, by using sub-questions that will allow them to demonstrate their qualifications (e.g., repeat a part of the question that the candidate seems to have omitted, ask if there is anything else to be added, remind the candidate of the number of expected components). Interviewers have a duty to search

2. Huffcutt and Arthur (1994). Also see Campion *et al.* (1997).
3. Eder and Harris (1999).

out all the information they need to evaluate the candidates, while preserving the objectivity of the process.[4] (See *Step 4, Respecting Certain Rules of Conduct.*)

FORMULATING QUESTIONS

Following are a few rules for formulating questions and preparing the interactions that will occur during the interview.[5] Several of the remarks and advice in this section were drawn from the experience of specialists, since there is little or no research on these aspects.

Rule 1 – Ask job-related questions. Questions and statements should have a direct link with the job or the selection criteria.

Rule 2 – Ask clear and precise questions. Questions and statements must be clear, precise and complete, while being as concise as possible. They must be written in language that is accessible to the candidate, and avoid vocabulary that only an insider could understand (e.g., government and public service jargon). Avoid double negatives.

Rule 3 – Make sure that the expected response is clear from the question. The questions must be sufficiently explicit for the candidate to understand the extent and direction of the expected response, in particular the length, and how many details or facts to include. Avoid asking vague questions that the candidate could respond to in several ways.

Example

Avoid: Discuss the concept of cost accounting. (Too vague)

Preferable: What conditions must be considered when establishing costs? (More explicit.)

---

4. Some decisions from the Quebec's Commission de la fonction publique support this point of view. (See the *Guide d'application des décisions de la Commission de la fonction publique*, p. 3-6.20–3-6.21 and 3-6.24).
5. See Pettersen (2000).

Rule 4 – Make sure the questions require complete and exact answers. For each question, it should be possible to determine what represents an exact and complete response. If you take the time to list the components of the expected responses, you will be able to detect the flaws in the question.

Rule 5 – Ask one question at a time. Each question must deal with one idea at a time. Several short and simple questions are preferable to one question made up of several parts.

Example

Avoid:	Which aspects of cost accounting do you handle best and which give you the greatest problem? (Two questions.)
Preferable:	Which aspects of cost accounting do you handle best?
	Which aspects of cost accounting give you the greatest problem? (One question at a time.)

Rule 6 – Don't give away the answer. The questions must not suggest the answer or dictate an obvious or desired response. Such questions are pointless and may even be harmful because they might let the candidate know which responses are expected.

Example

Avoid:	Are you the sort of person who's not afraid to put on your boots to inspect a job site? (Suggested response.)
Preferable:	When you inspect a job site, how do you go about it? (No suggested response.)

Rule 7 – Ask open questions. As far as possible, you should always ask **open** questions, which require a well-developed response. This enables interviewees to clarify their thoughts and establishes an atmosphere of communication that will allow them to express their ideas. In addition, too many **closed** questions (questions you can answer with a simple word such as "yes, no, never, four years," etc.) emphasize the competitive or test-like nature of the interview and may put the candidate on the defensive.

Example

Avoid: Did you react when your employee told you that he would not be ready for another week? (Closed question.)

Preferable: What did you do when your employee told you he would not be ready for another week? (Open question.)

Rule 8 – Ask non-threatening questions. As far as possible, your questions and interactions must not make the candidates uncomfortable or put them on the defensive. There are at least two reasons for this: *a*) to maintain a positive reaction on their part (review *Criteria for the Effectiveness of the Selection Interview*), and *b*) to encourage a climate of confidence, which will prompt them to open up more and reduce the likelihood of social desirability and forged answers. Questions that seem more threatening, annoying or personal may sometimes be asked, if it seems appropriate, but it is better not to ask them at the beginning of the interview; wait for the right moment.

Examples

a) Give an example of a situation in which you had to break your profession's code of ethics. (Threatening question.)

b) Give an example of a situation in which it was difficult to follow your profession's code of ethics to the letter. What did you do? (Less threatening question.)

Rule 9 – The level of difficulty must be job-appropriate. When you are dealing with questions that measure knowledge or skills, should you avoid questions that are very easy, so that nearly all the candidates will succeed, or very difficult, so most of them will fail? There are many considerations surrounding this issue. To keep it simple, we could say that the questions' level of difficulty must be representative of what is required for the job. You should not use questions that are easier or more difficult than those linked to the job. Therefore, even if a question seems relatively easy or hard, it should be included in the interview when the aspect it measures is an important component of the job.[6]

CONTENT OF THE QUESTIONS

Since interview questions are ways of gathering information from candidates, it is not surprising that their content correspond to various categories of indicators (see Table 2.2, *Indicator categories*). Questions may deal with:

- behaviours and results observable in the work situation (or taken from the candidate's previous history);
- behavioural intentions;
- technical and job-related knowledge;
- interests, motivations, aspirations, goals, opinions, attitudes; or,
- facts taken from the candidate's past history, such as training and experience.

The indicators relevant to the "Behaviours and results observable in the interview" category are observed without any particular question being prepared: they arise directly from the candidate's responses and behaviours during the interview and the only observation required is to make note of them (e.g., presents ideas in a structured way, takes initiative during the interview, earns the respect of the interviewers). Table 3.1 summarizes the relationship between the various kinds of questions and the nature of the indicators they measure.

6. See Pettersen (2000).

TABLE 3.1

Indicators measured by various types of questions

Indicators measured / Types of questions	Behaviours and results observable in the interview	Behaviours and results observable in the work situation	Behavioural intentions	Technical and job-related knowledge	Interests, motivations, goals, opinions, attitudes	Training and experience
Situational questions of the type "What would you do if...?"	✓		✓	✓		
Situational questions of the type "What is the best thing to do if...?"	✓			✓		
Behavioural questions	✓	✓		✓		
Knowledge questions	✓			✓		
Questions on training and experience	✓					✓
Willingness questions	✓		✓			
Questions on interests, goals and aspirations	✓				✓	
Questions on opinions and attitudes	✓				✓	
Self-evaluation questions	✓				✓	

MAIN TYPES OF QUESTIONS

There are a great variety of interview questions; some are more effective than others. Situational and behavioural questions are typical in the structured job-related interview, so we will pay particular attention to them.

A) Situational Questions ("What Would You Do If...? and "What Is the Best Thing to Do If...?")

Description. Popularized by Gary Latham and his colleagues around 1980, situational questions are written to put candidates in a hypothetical, but job-relevant situation, so that they can describe their future behaviour, or their **behavioural intentions.**[7] These are situational questions of the type, "**What would you do if...?**"

Sample questions for a department head's position

a) You have just returned from leave, and your assistant proudly announces that he has adopted a new file classification system. You know that the new system does not meet upper management requirements. What do you do?

b) You catch a colleague stealing office supplies. What do you do?

c) Two counter clerks who work together are openly critical of the employer, even in front of customers. You are afraid this negative attitude will spread to other employees. What do you do?

Adapted from *Les Affaires*, Saturday, April 15, 1989.

Technical or job-related knowledge. Even though situational questions of the "What would you do if...?" type deal with behavioural intentions, they can also reveal the candidate's knowledge. So candidates who respond well reveal two things: *a)* that they know how to act in that hypothetical situation, and *b)* that they have the knowledge

7. Eder and Harris (1999); Taylor and O'Driscoll (1995).

required to deal with this situation. However, the reciprocal is not necessarily true – if candidates give the wrong response, it does not necessarily mean that they do not know how to act. They can have the required knowledge without the intention of applying it. For example, a person may know that there is a regulation imposing a certain rule of behaviour, but answer that he or she would behave otherwise to deal with the situation.

If the situational questions are intended to measure **technical and job-related knowledge** rather than to gather behavioural intentions, it would be better to replace "What do you (or would you) do...?" with **"What is the best thing to do if...?"**[8]

Justification. Behavioural intentions make it possible to predict future behaviour because they reveal the objectives governing the candidate's actions in this kind of situation. According to Locke's motivation theory, behavioural intentions are the precursors of action.[9] It is important to give candidates several situations to deal with, in order to appreciate the consistency of their behavioural intentions. In the case of **knowledge**, research has shown that it represents one of the best predictors of job performance.[10]

Job-related situations. The more the situations reflect what actually happens on the job, the more the candidates' answers should represent their future behaviour. This is why it is strongly recommended that you base the situational questions on situations obtained by the **critical incident method** used in the job analysis.[11]

Real situational questions. Another way of going about it is to give candidates a situation that they may actually have to deal with if they are hired. After giving them enough details about the situation, ask them, "What **will you do** in this situation?" instead of "What would you do?"

---

8. Eder and Harris (1999).
9. Campion *et al.* (1997); Eder and Harris (1999).
10. Hunter (1986); Hunter and Hunter (1984); Schmidt and Hunter (1998).
11. Eder and Harris (1999); Taylor and O'Driscoll (1995).

Sample question for a chief of public works position

Many citizens are calling to complain of damage to their land caused by snow removal done by sub-contractors. What will you do to resolve this situation?

This approach was suggested by Eder and Harris (1999), who consider it most appropriate for complex situations or high-level jobs. This approach may also reduce the possibility of forged answers from candidates, who may believe that if they are hired, the committee members may remember what they said in the interview. (See *Social desirability and false answers.*)

Evaluating the responses. Ideally, situational questions are accompanied by a scoring guide that enables interviewers to evaluate the candidates' responses for each question. This kind of scoring guide should be based on the consensus of job experts: incumbents of a similar job, immediate superiors or any other person who knows the job. This may be prepared in a two-stage process. First, the experts are asked to draw up a list of all the possible responses, then to divide the points among those various expected response components, ensuring that the weighting is proportional to the importance of these components in the specific context of the job. The critical incidents gathered during the job analysis can be used to create the situations and the expected responses.

To evaluate the responses, **various approaches** can be used. We will describe three. The first works by **adding up points**: the points are divided among the expected response components and the candidates receive all the points corresponding to the components they provide (see Table 3.2). In this example, the candidate can accumulate points for several expected responses up to a maximum of 15 points.

The second method is one using **behavioural anchors**. The experts assign a value (e.g., 1, 3, or 5 points) to each of the expected responses. Several responses may have the same value. The expected responses are then sequenced to create a behaviourally anchored rating scale that will be used as the scoring guide – an example is found in Table 3.3. Here the candidate will be assigned a single point value for his or her

TABLE 3.2

Example of a scoring guide using the addition of points method

Criterion evaluated: *Consultation*
Job: Team leader

Question:
You are the head of a committee made up of various unit representatives. The committee has two months to make recommendations about the mission of a newly created agency. During the committee's first meeting, you realize that opposing opinions are being expressed. How are you doing to deal with this situation to achieve your objectives?

Expected response components (maximum 15 points):
- Understand all the positions well by clarifying each person's ideas (2 points)
- Determine the points of agreement with regard to the mission (3 points)
- Analyze each party's constraints (procedures, directions, deadlines, etc.) (1.5 point)
- Negotiate, convince (1.5 point)
- Suggest constructive compromises (2 points)
- Restate the objectives of the mandate and the planned timetable (1.5 point)
- Differentiate between the role of the decision maker and that of the person who makes recommendations (1.5 point)
- Demonstrate transparency, explain things (2 points)
- Any other relevant response

response based on whether it most resembles the ineffective responses (1 point), the average responses (3 points) or the effective responses (5 points).

Of these two methods, the addition of points method seems to be the most commonly used. However, we could use a **negative correction** to be fairer to the candidates: certain incorrect responses could make the candidate lose points. The candidates would have to be informed in advance that they would be penalized for wrong answers.

In contrast to the two previously discussed methods, in which the responses are evaluated question by question, there is a third method that consists of making the evaluation after the candidate has answered all the interview questions. In this case, there is no scoring guide for each question. The evaluation is done by **selection criteria**, based on the definitions of the selection criteria measured and their indicators, determined in *Step 2* (see Table 2.3). The evaluation by

TABLE 3.3

Example of a scoring guide with a behaviourally anchored rating scale

Criterion evaluated: *Human resources management*
Job: Head nurse

Question:
It is just before Christmas. Two nurses on your team call to tell you they will be absent as of tomorrow night, giving valid reasons. You will not have enough team members to do the job. How would you resolve this problem?

Expected responses:

1 point	The hospital has a pool of replacements. They should find staff to cover. *OR* There's nothing I can do about it. The private agency will take care of finding staff. *OR* I would tell the two nurses that they have to come to work. I wouldn't give them any choice.
3 points	I would discuss the situation with my manager. I would consider the possibility of moving a few patients to another ward or I would call the agency. *OR* I would try and convince the two nurses to arrange it between themselves so that only one would be absent, and I would fill the missing position with help from the agency.
5 points	I would discuss the situation with my manager. I would check to see if there might be any staff available from another ward. I would contact the agency to find out what the replacement possibilities are. If these possibilities fail, I would call on part-time or casual nurses. If I couldn't find any, I would consider the possibility of moving a few patients into another unit. If nothing else worked, I would replace one of the two nurses myself.

Adapted from Taylor and O'Driscoll (1995), p. 137–8.
Note: This method requires that the three response levels are mutually exclusive.

criteria method is described in *Step 5*, and an example of a rating scale is presented in Table 5.2. It should be noted that the behaviourally anchored method can also be applied to an evaluation by criteria, if more generic anchors relating to more than one question are used.

If this third method is used, the indicators can be determined before the questions are drawn up. On the other hand, if you use the addition of points or the behavioural anchors method, it seems more appropriate to establish indicators (expected response components) after preparing the questions.

Advantages (+) and Disadvantages (–) in Terms of the Four Main Criteria

We will now see how situational questions measure up in relation to the four effectiveness criteria described previously.

1. *Validity* (+). The observed validity for situational questions is one of the highest.[12] In addition, these questions are particularly resistant to bias on the part of interviewers (e.g., race, sex, age).[13]
2. *Reliability* (+). Reliability (agreement between evaluators) of situational questions is very high.[14]
3. *Compliance with the law and the organization's policies, as well as legal defensibility* (+). Situational questions are consistent with legal requirements because *a*) they are based on a job analysis, more specifically critical incidents, and *b*) they follow from evaluation components recognized by job experts.[15]
4. *Candidates' reactions* (+) (–). Most candidates react positively and are not very inclined to complain about the evaluation or to challenge it. However, if the interview only contains situational questions, some candidates may be disappointed, because they will have the impression that they did not have the opportunity to demonstrate all their qualifications, particularly with regard to their motivation.[16]

---

12. Eder and Harris (1999); Taylor and O'Driscoll (1995).
13. Eder and Harris (1999).
14. Eder and Harris (1999); Gatewood and Feild (2001); Taylor and O'Driscoll (1995).
15. See Eder and Harris (1999).
16. See Eder and Harris (1999).

Other Advantages (+) and Disadvantages (–)

1. *Creation of the questions* (–). Preparing situational questions is a lengthy and expensive process, given the need to call on several experts to do the job analysis by critical incidents and to write the scoring guide. In addition, the entire process must be supervised by human resources specialists. Consequently, creating situational questions is cost-effective only to the extent that these questions can be used with many candidates.[17]
2. *Ease of application* (+). Once they have been written, situational questions are easy to use in an interview and they have an undeniable advantage for less experienced interviewers when it comes to response evaluation.[18]
3. *Jobs targeted* (+) (–). The questions may apply to a wide range of jobs. On the other hand, they are less suitable to new positions or those that only have a few employees, because it will be difficult to find enough experts to gather many critical incidents or write the expected responses for these jobs.[19]
4. *Candidates targeted* (+). Situational questions are suitable for all types of candidates. They are particularly appropriate for entry-level positions where the candidates do not have a lot of experience. Since these questions deal with behavioural intentions or knowledge, a candidate can respond correctly, even without relevant experience. On the other hand, compared to behavioural questions, situational questions seem to have a lower predictive validity when used for high-level positions.[20] In these circumstances, especially when candidates have a great deal of experience, the situational questions must be sufficiently complex to allow interviewers to identify the most competent candidates.
5. *Social desirability and forged answers* (–). Situational questions of the "what do you do if...?" type, written to obtain **behavioural intentions,** have one major failing. What candidates say they will do in a hypothetical situation that relates to their values or a

17. Taylor and O'Driscoll (1995).
18. Taylor and O'Driscoll (1995).
19. Eder and Harris (1999); Taylor and O'Driscoll (1995).
20. Huffcutt, Weekley, Wiesner, Degroot, and Jones (2001); Pulakos *et al.* (1996).

moral judgment does not necessarily have a strong correlation to what they would actually do in a work context.[21] A person applying for a job probably wants to get the job very much, so their responses may be subject to a **social desirability** – a tendency to give answers that are more acceptable to society in general and the organization in particular. Some go so far as to give **false responses.** So for a problem that requires a firm but delicate decision (e.g., dealing with an employee who has stolen something), candidates will probably respond that they will fulfill the responsibilities of the position. But will they do so in a real work situation, when the employee is a close friend, a colleague, or someone they owe something to?

If candidates give the right response, however, the evaluator can deduce from this that they have the relevant **knowledge**, whether or not they are trying to mask their real intentions or will act differently later. In other words, they at least know what the right thing to do is.

6. *Interviewers' reactions* (–). Some interviewers may have a negative reaction to an interview that only contains situational questions. The interview may be viewed as too constraining.[22] Don't forget, however, that sub-questions are entirely possible; these are in fact the main advantage of using interviews rather than written tests.

B) Behavioural Questions ("Give an Example of...")

Description. Behavioural questions first appeared in the 1960s, but they were really developed twenty years later by Tom Janz (1982), who called the technique *behavioural description interviewing.*[23] The resulting interview method has been given various names: *targeted* or *focused selection*, or *behavioural interviewing.*[24] Aimed at **past and observable behaviour in a work situation,** behavioural questions require the candidate to describe what he or she did in a past situation more or less similar to a situation that might arise in the job at issue.[25]

21. Campion *et al.* (1997); Eder and Harris (1999); Pettersen (2000).
22. See Eder and Harris (1999).
23. Taylor and O'Driscoll (1995).
24. Revenue Canada (1992).
25. Eder and Harris (1999).

Examples

a) Can you give a precise example of a time you went beyond your normal duties to help a customer?

b) Tell us about the last time you had to reprimand a subordinate.

c) Give us an instance when you were not able to meet a high-priority deadline.

d) How do you act when you have to deal with an angry customer? Give an example.

Technical or job-related knowledge. It is entirely possible to use behavioural questions to measure technical or job-related knowledge. You just need to ask the candidate to give examples of behaviour that allow you to verify this knowledge.[26]

Examples

a) Can you give three examples of situations that demonstrate your mastery of tax law?

b) Tell us about times when your knowledge of Windows software was inadequate.

Justification. **Knowledge**, as we have seen previously, constitutes one of the best predictors of job performance. **Past behaviours** predict future behaviours because they reveal the choices a person has made and therefore describe his or her usual patterns of behaviour.[27] For example, when candidates describe a precise situation where, as a customer service agent, they knew how to deal effectively with an angry customer, you can infer that they would act similarly with another unsatisfied customer if they were in a similar job. This actually is a verification of references, in a way, but the information comes from the candidates themselves.[28]

26. Taylor and O'Driscoll (1995).
27. Campion *et al.* (1997); Eder and Harris (1999); Taylor and O'Driscoll (1995).
28. Canada Revenue Agency (1992).

To evaluate the **consistency** of a person's behaviour, it seems important to ask for more than one example of behaviour or situation per selection criterion. In theory, three examples of behaviour per criterion would be the minimum.[29] But in practice, we often have to limit ourselves to two, in order to avoid taking too much time for the interview or having to reduce the number of criteria measured. (See *Length of the Interview and Number of Questions, infra.*)

Job-related questions. The situation described by the candidate must be relevant to the job in question, without necessarily being identical.[30] To clarify that, we will suppose that a man without work experience applies for a clerk's position for which "Organization" has been established as one of the selection criteria. During the interview, he cites the example of an overwhelming daily-life situation (e.g., renovating his home, taking his children to their activities) and demonstrates all the behaviours expected of an organized person. Can we say that the example is not relevant because it was not taken from a work situation? The complexity level of the situation in the person's example must be taken into consideration – if the complexity is representative of the kind of situations that a clerk would face, then the example may be considered appropriate. For instance, the situation above would probably not be acceptable for a senior manager's position.

The three components of a behavioural example. Behavioural questions allow you to obtain a description of a past behaviour. However, in order for the interviewer to really understand a person's past behaviour, the example must present the following three aspects:

a) the **situation** which led to the candidate's actions, or in which the actions took place;

b) the candidate's specific **actions**; and

c) the **results** or consequences that ensued from the actions.

29. Eder and Harris (1999).
30. Byham (1987); Taylor and O'Driscoll (1995).

To be complete, each description of past behaviour should include these three components.[31] As a result, the interviewer shall usually adopt a **two-stage approach**: formulation of the main question, and then, if necessary, prompting questions.[32]

Main questions. The previous examples correspond to main questions that usually begin like this:[33]

- Tell us about an experience in which...
- What has been your experience with...
- Describe a situation in which...
- Give an example of...
- When did you feel most satisfied with your ability to...

If the objective is to gather facts and behaviours, as is the case with behavioural questions, you should avoid questions such as, "What would you do if you had to do it again?" or "What would you do if you were in this situation?"[34] On the other hand, it may be appropriate to ask these kinds of questions if you want to ask about the knowledge a candidate has acquired after an experience, as long as you do not forget that you are getting behavioural intentions and opinions.

Prompting questions for a partially described behaviour. After asking the main question, the interviewer must verify whether the candidate's response includes the three necessary components (situation, actions, results) in order to be a complete behavioural example. Since most every response only includes one or two of these components, the interviewer should move on to prompting questions that allow the behavioural example to be completed. Following are some examples of this kind of question.[35]

31. Byham (1987).
32. Byham (1987).
33. Adapted from Canada Revenue Agency (1992).
34. Taylor and O'Driscoll (1995)
35. Taken in part from Byham (1987), chap. 8, p. 3–4, and from Revenue Canada (1992), p. A-1–A-13.

For the *situation* component, the prompting question might be:

- Can you describe the situation?
- What were the circumstances of this event or its context?
- What was the cause of...?
- Why did you...?
- What were the other factors that made you...?
- When did that happen...?
- Who was involved?
- How much time did it take you to act?

For the *actions* component, the prompting questions could be:

- What did you do exactly?
- Can you describe exactly the steps you took?
- What was your reaction?
- What else did you do?
- What was your role in this situation?
- What was your contribution in this situation?
- What was the contribution of others in this situation?

For the *results* component, the prompting questions could be:

- What was the result of...?
- What did that do to...?
- How did that affect...?
- What were the reactions from...?

It is important to clarify the candidate's real contribution in relation to the other people concerned. Some candidates have a tendency to take credit for actions that were not theirs.

Prompting questions and standardization. Prompting questions allow interviewers to get all the information relating to a behavioural example. However, these questions can affect the level of standardization (structure) of the interviews and be detrimental to the equal treatment of all candidates. For example, a selection committee may meet with a rather talkative candidate who provides complete and detailed responses. In this case, the committee members may think they have all the information they need, and therefore not ask any prompting questions. Afterwards the committee may meet a more reserved candidate who gives brief responses, so the committee must ask several prompting questions. Even though the two interviews were different, this lack of standardization has no serious consequences with respect to the two candidates having the opportunity to provide complete responses, that is, responses clarifying the situation, actions and results. If, however, the talkative candidate gives a detailed response, but one that is incomplete as to his or her actions, the committee, impressed with the large quantity of information provided, might not deem it necessary to ask probing questions that would allow the candidate to complete the response. In this case, one might allege a lack of equity.

To avoid this situation, the interviewer or one of the selection committee members could take notes during the interview using a question sheet such as those in Tables 3.4 and 3.5. It would then be easy

TABLE 3.4

**Sample question sheet 1:
Two behavioural questions and their related prompting questions**

Criterion evaluated: *Leadership*

Main question:
Give an example of an instance during the last few months when you acted firmly with one of your employees.

Prompting questions:
- When did that happen?
- What was the situation?
- What did you do exactly?
- How did the others react?

Main question:
It sometimes happens that we need the help of people who are not under our authority. Can you give an example where you had to obtain the cooperation of a group outside your unit?

Prompting questions:
- When did that happen?
- What was the context?
- What exactly did you do to influence them?
- How did the members of this group react?
- What was the result?

TABLE 3.5

Sample question sheet 2: Two behavioural questions with situation, actions and results headings to direct the prompting

Criterion evaluated: *Leadership*
Give an example of an instance during the last few months when you acted firmly with one of your employees. - Situation: - Actions: - Results:
It sometimes happens that we need the help of people who are not under our authority. Can you give an example where you had to obtain the cooperation of a group outside your unit? - Situation: - Actions: - Results:

to check and see that all three components of a behavioural example (situation, actions and results) have been described. Of course, if you maintain a high level of concentration during the interview, you will also be able to ensure that the responses cover all three aspects. This responsibility can be divided among the members of the committee (e.g., the person who asks the questions is responsible for making sure that all these components are covered). In the case of a very structured interview, the candidates could be given a written list of behavioural questions, including the prompting questions, and be told that it is their responsibility to provide all the information required. After each question, they could also be asked to verify that their response is complete.

Prompting questions for an incorrect response. Sometimes the candidate's response does not describe facts or behaviours but rather an opinion, feeling, interest, or behavioural intention. In addition, the response does not always specify what the person did, or what happened. The interviewer then has to encourage the candidate to provide a real behavioural example with the aid of prompting questions.

Examples of prompting questions for a response in the form of an opinion

Response: I think it's important to act quickly in this kind of situation.

Questions: What did you do exactly?

How much time did it take you to act?

Examples of prompting questions for vague responses

Response: I usually act quickly when a problem arises.

Questions: Can you tell us about the last time this happened?

Give a specific example of what happened.

A useful exercise for practising how to recognize and obtain a true and complete behaviour description is presented in Appendix G.

Positive, negative and neutral behaviour. The main questions can deal with examples of positive, negative or neutral behaviour. To promote a better atmosphere during the interview, it seems preferable not to begin with negative ones.

Examples

a) Tell us about the most recent time you were able to influence a major decision in your unit. (Positive.)

b) Give us an example of a time when you were unable to meet a high-priority deadline (Negative.)

c) How do you deal with an angry customer? Give us an example. (Neutral.)

In practice, many candidates evade questions to which they must give negative examples, claiming that they have never encountered that kind of problem, but other candidates, more open, or perhaps more honest, do answer these questions. Committee members may put too much importance on the negative examples when they are making an evaluation, which penalizes the more honest candidates in comparison to the ones who preferred not to answer. This is no doubt the reason why some interviewers prefer not to ask for negative examples.

Lists of prepared questions. Lists of ready-made behavioural questions for various selection criteria are available.[36] They make it much easier to prepare an interview, especially when you do not have a lot of experience with this type of question.

Tables 3.4 and 3.5 above show two examples of behavioural questions related to the "Leadership" criterion. In the first example, each main question is accompanied by prompting questions. However, when preparing an interview, it is not absolutely essential to plan for prompting questions in this way. Experienced interviewers can use an interview guide that only includes the main questions and the following headings: – Situation, – Actions, – Results. (See *Writing the Interview Guide, infra.*)

Evaluating rcsponses. Even though it is possible to write a scoring guide specifying the expected response components for each of the behavioural questions, method is rarely used. Most of the time, during the interview, questions are simply grouped by selection criteria. After the interview, the candidates are evaluated by criteria, according to the behaviour examples they provided: quantity, recent nature of the behaviours, relevance to the job, effectiveness, etc.[37] Of course, the evaluation is done with the help of pre-established indicators for each criterion (see *Step 2, Determining the Indicators or Expected Responses*). In principle, a behavioural question only deals with a single selection criterion. However, a question may cause candidates to provide a description of behaviours which belong to more than one criterion. Therefore, these behaviours must be correctly classified during the evaluation. (See *Step 5, Evaluation by Criteria.*) In situations requiring a very structured process, each behavioural question should only deal

---

36. See, for example: Byham (1987), under "Prepared Questions"; Canada Revenue Agency (1992), Appendix A; Taylor and O'Driscoll (1995), Appendix F.
37. Byham (1987); Taylor and O'Driscoll (1995).

with a single criterion and could include a scoring guide containing expected response components such as the guide suggested for the situational questions.

Advantages (+) and Disadvantages (–) in Relation to the Four Main Criteria

1. *Validity* (+). Although it is generally agreed that the validity of behavioural questions is particularly high, some studies assign a higher validity to situational questions.[38] For now, it is difficult to give a definite opinion. However, behavioural questions have a lower correlation to mental aptitudes than situational questions, which should give an advantage to their marginal contribution when they are used in combination with a mental aptitude test.[39]

2. *Reliability* (+). The reliability (agreement between evaluators) of behavioural questions seems to be very high.[40] It may be slightly lower than the reliability of situational questions,[41] but the research does not support a definitive stance on this issue.[42] Using a standardized scoring guide should increase the degree of reliability.

3. *Compliance with the law and the organization's policies, as well as legal defensibility* (+) (–). Used in the Canada's federal public service, behavioural questions have been the subject of several appeals by candidates, and the majority of these appeals have been dismissed.[43] An analysis of the decisions rendered shows that behavioural questions are defensible when:

   a) the questions are well constructed, and prompting questions are used;

   b) the information gathered can be verified by other methods (i.e., consulting references);

   c) the interviewers have been trained to use this technique.

---

38. See Campion *et al.* (1997); Eder and Harris (1999); Gatewood and Feild (2001); Taylor and O'Driscoll 1995).
39. See Gatewood and Feild (2001); Eder and Harris (1999).
40. See Gatewood and Feild (2001).
41. See Eder and Harris (1999).
42. Campion *et al.* (1997).
43. Out of seven appeals reported by Canada Revenue Agency (1992), behavioural questions were deemed inappropriate in only two cases.

4. *Candidates' reaction* (+). Candidates generally consider that this approach is fair and believe it gives them the opportunity to demonstrate their competence.[44]

Other advantages (+) and Disadvantages (–)

1. *Development* (+) (–). Writing behavioural questions is simple and quick as long as each not accompanied by a scoring guide.[45] It is not necessary to obtain the participation of personnel specialists to supervise the whole approach. However, developing a scoring guide is a long and costly process, as it is for situational questions.
2. *Ease of application* (–). Once they are prepared, behavioural questions require a certain skill from the interviewer because he or she must ensure follow-up with prompting questions.[46] In addition, responses are generally more difficult to evaluate.
3. *Jobs targeted* (+). Behavioural questions can apply to almost any kind of job.
4. *Candidates targeted* (+) (–). Behavioural questions are particularly suitable for candidates who have relevant experience and who will be in a position to provide behaviour examples related to the job.[47] A candidate without experience may be at a disadvantage. However, for people who have less experience, the questions may be broadened to other experiences, even including behaviour outside the work sphere. It is also important to be careful not to give priority to the quantity of behaviour examples at the expense of their quality.[48]
5. *Social desirability and forged answers* (+). It is hard to know just how far candidates might distort their responses in order to be seen in a better light, but we believe that using past behaviours reduces

44. Canada Revenue Agency (1992).
45. Taylor and O'Driscoll (1995).
46. Taylor and O'Driscoll (1995).
47. Eder and Harris (1999).
48. Gatewood and Feild (2001).

the risk of being fooled. It is hard for the candidate to continue inventing responses, especially if the interviewer asks for details on the circumstances and the actions taken.[49]

6. *Interviewers' reactions* (+) (–). Faced with behavioural questions, interviewers always have positive reactions. As with situational questions, however, some may feel limited by an interview that is only composed of behavioural questions. The use of other questions must therefore be considered.

Which questions to choose: situational or behavioural? Is it better to ask candidates "what they would do" (situational question) than "what they did" (behavioural question)? There is no straightforward answer to that. To resolve this issue, you need to review, for each situation and its context, the advantages and disadvantages of the two types of questions relative to the criteria presented above. Both types of questions are allowable, but combining the two types can result in other complications when evaluating. We usually use a question-based evaluation system for the situational questions and a criteria-based system for behavioural questions (see *Step 5*). However, if the evaluation of the behavioural questions is done by questions, each behavioural question dealing only with a single selection criterion, it is easy to use situational questions and behavioural questions in the same interview.

A practical guide on how to prepare situational and behavioural questions can be found in Appendix E and an exercise on writing them is available in Appendix F.

C) Knowledge Questions

Description. Knowledge questions deal with the **technical or job-related knowledge** required by the position. There are two sorts of knowledge questions: those that require candidates to **describe** their knowledge, and those that require them to **demonstrate** it.[50] Questions in the second category are similar to written test questions, and they certainly represent a more reliable way of verifying knowledge.

49. Byham (1987); Eder and Harris (1999).
50. Campion *et al.* (1997).

Examples of questions requiring a description

a) Can you tell us what you know about tax law?

b) Tell us what software programs you are fully competent to use.

c) What kind of car can you drive?

Examples of questions requiring a demonstration

a) Which sections of the *Taxation Act* apply to inheritance?

b) How do you produce a histogram in Excel?

c) What is the critical incident method and how is it applied in the context of selection?

d) In a selection interview, what distinguishes situational questions from behavioural questions?

Justification. Research has demonstrated that knowledge not only predicts job performance but is also one of the best performance predictors.[51]

Situational and behavioural questions. As mentioned above, situational and behavioural questions are very well suited to knowledge evaluation, because they require a demonstration. (See *Situational Questions* and *Behavioural Questions.*)

Scoring guide. Ideally, to obtain a precise and objective evaluation of knowledge, you need a structured scoring guide that contains the expected response components. This kind of guide should be drawn up like the ones for situational or behavioural questions. (See *Situational Questions* and *Behavioural Questions.*)

51. Hunter (1986); Hunter and Hunter (1984); Schmidt and Hunter (1998).

D) Questions on Training and Experience

Description. Questions on training and experience (background questions) deal with the candidates' past history and provide information about their education, work or other relevant experience, formal upgrading courses, etc. (See table 2.2, *Indicator categories.*)[52]

Examples

a) What degrees, diplomas and other qualifications do you have to work in the personnel selection field?

b) What training have you had on the selection interview?

c) What kind of practical experience have you had with personnel selection?

d) Up to now, what have been your main responsibilities in personnel selection?

e) Who made the hiring decisions and how were they made?

f) Which are your favorite reference books on personnel selection?

Justification. First of all, training and experience tells you that the person probably has a certain level of knowledge, an essential factor in job performance. (See *Step 2, Determining the Indicators or Expected Responses.*) Second, experience is an important source of behaviour drawn from the person's past, and as with behavioural questions, these past behaviours predict future behaviours in similar situations. Furthermore, if they are very specific, questions on experience can end up resembling behavioural questions.

Advantages of asking training and experience questions in the interview. It is true that most of the information gathered with these questions could be obtained from a detailed résumé or an appropriate job application form. However, asking these questions in an interview has certain advantages: *a*) it is a good way to start the interview, *b*) it allows for clarification or completion of the résumé, and *c*) it gives

52. Campion *et al.* (1997); Eder and Harris (1999).

candidates the opportunity to demonstrate their qualifications, which increases the likelihood that their reactions to the interview will be positive.[53]

E) Willingness Questions

Description. These questions allow you to discuss the candidates' availability directly with them: are they ready to perform certain tasks, respond to certain requirements or work in a certain context? It is interesting to note that these questions are, in fact, actual situational questions. (See *Situational Questions.*) Therefore they deal with **behavioural intentions.**

Examples

a) This job has a very strict schedule. No unjustified lateness will be tolerated, since the employees who are at work will have to do the job until you arrive. To what extent are you ready to accept these conditions?

b) What is your reaction to having to work a Saturday and a Sunday once a month?

c) Sometimes customers get very angry and they can be violent, using insults, threats and even occasionally attempting physical violence. Of course, there is always a security officer on site. Are you sure you want this job?

Justification. Although there do not seem to be studies dealing with the effectiveness of this kind of question, two considerations may be put forth to warrant their use. First, since these questions deal with behavioural intentions, we can use the same justification as for situational questions. Second, these questions help provide the candidate with a realistic description of the job. Studies have demonstrated that a realistic job description increases the satisfaction of the people hired and decreases employee turnover.[54]

53. Eder and Harris (1999).
54. Breaugh (2000); Haccoun, Rigny and Bordeleau (1979).

Evaluation of responses. These questions can be asked in a preselection interview or in a hiring interview. The candidate's responses do not always need to be evaluated.

F) Questions on Interests, Objectives and Aspirations

Description. These questions target the candidate's motivation. They concern work **interests, objectives** and **aspirations** regarding the position to be filled.

Examples

a) Which parts of your current job do you like the best?

b) What makes a job motivating for you?

c) What kind of boss do you like best?

d) If you could do it over again, what field would you study?

e) What job would you like to have in five years?

G) Questions on Opinions and Attitudes

Description. Questions concerning **opinions** and **attitudes** aim at understanding what the candidate thinks about job-related subjects.

Examples

a) Many people say that meetings are a waste of time. What is your opinion about the usefulness of meetings?

b) Do you think that in certain situations it is better not to follow the rules laid down by the company?

c) What do you think the minister's role should be in relation to his senior bureaucrats?

d) What do you think about young people's motivation for work?

H) Self-evaluation Questions

Description. These questions allow you to find out what candidates think of themselves. They are also questions about **opinions**, in a way.

Examples

a) What makes you a good candidate for this job?

b) What are your greatest strengths?

c) As an employee, which aspects should you improve?

d) If we met the people you work with and asked them how they would like you to improve, which aspects do you think they would mention?

I) Recommended Types of Questions

No type of question is perfect. However, certain questions are intrinsically better than others. These are *a*) situational questions, *b*) behavioural questions, *c*) knowledge questions, *d*) questions about training and experience and *e*) willingness questions. These all tend to be more structured and job-related.

Questions on interests, objectives and aspirations, questions on opinions and attitudes and self-evaluation questions are generally less structured and give rise to social desirability and forged answers. In addition, no research has been made on their validity. They are probably less valid and reliable, and it would be difficult to defend them in the case of a challenge, so they should be used with great caution.[55]

J) The Interview Architect

Description. There is a form of interview called the "Interview Architect."[56] It uses various kinds of questions and ensures a high predictive validity. This form of interview allows you to evaluate each selection criterion using a four-part approach. The four components are:

55. Eder and Harris (1999).
56. Durivage and Thibault (2000); Lombardo and Eichinger (1995).

1. *Has already done.* This component, which is similar to the behavioural approach, aims at obtaining descriptions of what the candidate has done recently in situations that are relevant to the selection criteria evaluated. Following the established categories of indicators, these questions may specifically target either behaviours and outcomes that are observable in the work situation, or knowledge.

Example

Can you describe a situation in which you demonstrated tact and diplomacy – when someone contradicted you or criticized you, for instance? What were the circumstances? How did you handle it? What were the results?

2. *Has observed.* This component examines what the candidate was able to learn by observing people who have fulfilled the selection criteria being evaluated. The type of question used is based on the premise that part of our competency is acquired by observing and imitating others. As with the behavioural questions, these questions deal with past behaviours, positive or negative, that are attributable to a person other than the interviewee. However, the indicators thus obtained are limited to knowledge indicators.

Example

Do you know a person who is particularly diplomatic? What characterizes this person? How does he or she act in general? Give an example of a time when this person had to intervene in a conflict situation. What were the circumstances? What did the person do? What was the result?

3. *Has understood.* Like the preceding component, this one aims mainly at knowledge indicators. It includes knowledge and situational questions that are intended to evaluate the extent to which the candidate understands how a particular competence or quality works: how it is learned, why it is necessary, how you put it into practice, etc. Understanding how a competence functions increases the chance of using it effectively and being able to teach it to other people.

Example

Define in your own terms what it means to act with tact and diplomacy. What distinguishes a person who shows tact from a person who is lacking it? How can we develop these qualities? In what circumstances are these qualities particularly required? How do you go about showing tact and diplomacy in a difficult interpersonal situation?

4. *Has mastered.* The purpose of this last component is to learn the candidate's opinion of his own competencies and personal qualities. The questions used, which are of the self-evaluation type, make it possible to obtain opinion indicators.

Example

Are you tactful and diplomatic? In comparison with others, are you more, less or equally diplomatic? What are your strong points in this area? Which aspects can you improve?

Scoring guide. With this form of interview, the responses obtained are evaluated by selection criteria (see *Step 5, Evaluation by Criteria*), using definitions and indicators suggested in the "Interview Architect" model.

COMMUNICATION TECHNIQUES AND WAYS OF ASKING QUESTIONS

There are several ways of communicating with candidates and asking them questions. Depending on the interview procedure and its context, certain methods are more appropriate than others. Among the techniques presented in this section, some may be used right away for developing the interview guide; others may only be used during the interview.[57]

57. This section is adapted from an unpublished document by Roland Foucher, professor at the Université du Québec en Outaouais.

1. *Introduction questions.* Introduction questions are asked when a new subject is being approached; they invite the candidate to cover various general topics. They are open questions that usually require the candidates to structure their response. Introduction questions should not be too broad.

Examples

a) Can you describe in some detail the responsibilities you have in this position?

b) Can you tell us what you know about tax law?

2. *Simple recall questions.* These questions are used to gather a large quantity of information, most frequently factual information. They are often closed questions.

Examples

a) What methods do you use to do the follow-up on your files?

b) How many employees are you directly responsible for?

3. *Multiple-choice questions.* By offering the candidate various response choices, multiple-choice questions have several uses: *a*) they can verify a very specific hypothesis, *b*) they facilitate the candidate's understanding of a complex question, and *c*) they allow a candidate who is not a talker to prepare a response more easily.

Examples

a) In a selection interview, what distinguishes situational questions from behavioural questions? Is it: 1) their validity; 2) the difficulty with which they are applied; or 3) what they measure in the candidates?

b) Could you tell us what gave you the most satisfaction in your latest jobs? (*To facilitate a hesitant candidate's ability to reflect on this question, the interviewer adds the choice of the following responses.*) For example, some people get the most satisfaction from their wages, or their job security; others like the opportunity for promotion or interesting tasks. What gives you the most satisfaction, personally?

4. *Double-edged questions.* This kind of question offers a choice of two responses; one of them is stated in such a way that very few candidates can choose it. People will opt for the second choice, which will act as a kind of entry for the interviewer to ask some prompting questions. This type of question is difficult to write and is best prepared prior to the interview. They should not be used often, because they can put the candidate on the defensive.

Example

Are you always as firm as you would like to be, or could this aspect be improved? (Once the candidate has chosen the second response, the interviewer can ask the following prompting questions.) Can you tell us more about it? Give us a recent example.

5. *Indirect questions.* Indirect questions ask candidates to talk about themselves by proxy. They are less compromising and can make it easier for candidates to discuss aspects that are very close to them. These questions can also reduce social desirability and forged answers since the candidate does not know whether the other people concerned will really be consulted in a possible reference check.

Examples

a) If we met with the people who work with you and asked them how you should improve, what aspects would they mention?

b) In your last performance appraisal, what were the strong points and aspects needing improvement mentioned by your boss?

6. *Confrontational questions.* When candidates give a very general response, or one that seems exaggerated, they should be asked to give concrete examples, as is the case with behavioural questions. However, these questions are to be avoided at the beginning of the interview, so as not to put the candidate on the defensive.

7. *Pauses and silences.* Silences should not be broken automatically. They may indicate that the person *a)* needs more time for reflection, *b)* is hesitant to mention something, *c)* is resting momentarily, or *d)* just does not want to answer a problematic question. A pause or a silence on the interviewer's part is an invitation to the interviewee to develop his or her ideas. After a few seconds, if the candidate says nothing more, you need to verify what is going on (e.g., "Is everything OK?" or "Shall I let you think about it a little longer?"). Some people have a tendency to answer very quickly in an interview, probably to make themselves look better to the interviewer, so you need to let them know that they can take their time.[58] Sometimes, however, interviewers should show that they are in control, keeping the pressure on with their silence (e.g., when the person gives a vague answer to a problematic question). Silence must not be abused, though, since it may create undue tension in the interviewee.

Example

Interviewer:	What do you do to stay up-to-date in your field?
Candidate:	I read a lot. And I always go to the annual meetings of the Society for Industrial and Organizational Psychology.
Interviewer:	(*Confrontation.*) I'd like to know what kind of books you read. Could you tell me what you've read recently?
Candidate:	Yes, I read Guion's latest book on personnel selection. And I subscribe to *Personnel Psychology.*
Interviewer:	(*Confrontation.*) Which articles had the most effect on you recently?

58. Canada Revenue Agency (1992).

Other Communication Techniques

The following techniques belong more to the clinical interview, preferably done by psychologists or other behaviour specialists. These techniques require the interviewer to interpret the candidate's responses, which they may do incorrectly, or they may suggest other avenues of response to the candidate. In most cases, it is wise to avoid these techniques and just ask prompting questions of the "Can you give us more details?" or "Can you tell us more?" type.

1. *Restatement.* Restatement deals with the obvious substance of the candidates' remarks. It is generally brief and consists of *a*) summarizing what the candidate said, *b*) picking up on one particular point, or *c*) simply reproducing the final words so as to facilitate the continuation of the discussion. It helps establish an atmosphere in which the interviewee has a feeling of being supported and not being observed.

Examples

a)	Interviewer:	Do you expect to encounter some difficulties when you start this new job?
	Candidate:	The only difficulty I expect is that I would work more slowly at the beginning. At least until I know better how you go about things.
	Interviewer:	(*Restatement.*) If I understand correctly, you have a tendency to begin slowly, but pick up speed as you begin to understand your duties.
	Candidate:	Yes, I think that's it. I like to be sure of myself before taking charge of an activity. And what I was doing before is not exactly the same as the job you are offering...
b)	Candidate:	I think you can say that on my last project, I definitely succeeded.
	Interviewer:	(*Restatement.*) You mean, the results were satisfactory.
	Candidate:	That's right. First of all, everybody was happy...

2. *Reflecting feelings.* This technique aims at drawing out feelings, intentions or any other thoughts that are behind the candidate's words, to suggest rather than impose ways of pursuing these ideas.

Examples

a)	Candidate:	(*In a louder voice.*) I warned them, but they didn't listen to me.
	Interviewer:	(*Reflecting feelings.*) Just thinking about it seems to make you angry.
	Candidate:	You're right. I had worked very hard and I was very sure I was right. But they never take our opinions into account...
b)	Candidate:	It's always the same people who get a pat on the back in this company.
	Interviewer:	(*Reflecting feelings.*) And you don't like that.
	Candidate:	Exactly.
	Interviewer:	(*Reflecting feelings.*) You feel hurt.
	Candidate:	It's always been the same. You know, it's not necessarily the best employees who are popular with the bosses. I'm saying that some people just know how to look good.

3. *Elucidation.* Clarification consists of identifying ideas that do not follow directly from the candidate's words, but may reasonably be deduced from the remarks or their context. It requires a certain intellectual acuity.

Example

Candidate:	It was one of my colleagues. In a meeting, he was always the one who talked. As soon as he arrived, there was nothing else to be done, no way of getting a word in edgewise.
Interviewer:	(*Restatement.*) He was the one who always took over the meeting?

Candidate:	Yes, exactly.
Interviewer:	(*Reflecting feelings.*) And that bothered you?
Candidate:	It depends. In the beginning, it didn't, because I admired this person, but in the end, I couldn't stand him. I ended up taking it personally, you know.
Interviewer:	(*Elucidation.*) You mean you had the impression that this person didn't consider you at all, that you felt diminished in his presence, is that right?

PREPARING AND SEQUENCING THE QUESTIONS

Now that you are in possession of all the knowledge and techniques presented in the first part of *Step 3*, you are ready to prepare the interview **questions** in accordance with the structured job-related interview approach. However, on the basis of the level of structure chosen, whether it be level 3 or slightly below level 4, the interviewer has a certain flexibility during the interview to adapt questions, ask prompting questions or modify the sequence slightly. (See *Standardizing the Questions and Their Sequence.*)

It is important to organize the questions in a logical sequence, so the candidates and the selection committee members can follow the thread. This sequence must also be appropriate for obtaining the information needed and relevant for the chosen selection criteria. Several sequences are possible.[59]

1. *In chronological order.* The questions are simply organized in the order of the sequence of events over time, beginning with the earliest. In a way, candidates are asked to tell their stories. This sequence, typical of the traditional interview, gives the interviewer a better grasp of the relationship between events and a better understanding of the candidate's professional and personal development. In addition, the sequence of the interview is more like a natural conversation, which may help create an atmosphere of confidence in which the candidate is less defensive.

59. Campion *et al.* (1997); Eder and Harris (1999).

Application: A very useful sequence for examining aspects of the candidate's résumé, like education and training, and work experience.

2. *By selection criteria.* The questions are grouped according to the various selection criteria. This way, the information gathered from the candidate will already be organized according to the aspects to be evaluated, which will also facilitate the analysis and evaluation process. This is an important advantage for interviewers and selection committee members who are not interview specialists.

   Application: The most practical sequence for situational, behavioural and knowledge questions.

3. *By job tasks and responsibilities.* The questions are grouped according to the main components of the job (e.g., tasks, responsibilities or functions). If the selection criteria are themselves modeled on the job components, this sequence is as advantageous as the previous one.

   Application: May be interesting for situational and behavioural questions, and sometimes knowledge questions.

Recommended Combination of Sequences

These different methods of organizing the questions in a logical sequence can be combined in various ways, from one interview to another, or within one interview. For example, the interview questions could be organized in three parts:[60] first, the questions on education and experience in chronological order (most interviewees expect this way of beginning, which makes them comfortable); then, situational, behavioural and knowledge questions, in order of the selection criteria or job components; and finally, the willingness questions, asked in relation to job components.

60. Eder and Harris (1999).

LENGTH OF THE INTERVIEW AND NUMBER OF QUESTIONS

To be **valid**, an interview must contain enough questions to ensure that all the required information is gathered, so that each of the necessary selection criteria for the job can be evaluated.[61] It is important to verify this, which can be done quickly when the questions are grouped according to selection criteria. However, when the questions are organized in chronological order or according to job components, it is desirable to do this verification with a "questions by criteria" two-way table, or at least by indicating the selection criteria targeted for each question.

To be **reliable**, an interview must contain a minimum number of questions. Theoretically, the more questions there are, the more reliable the interview. But in practice, you have to deal with time constraints and the effects of fatigue.

So how many questions should it be limited to? An interview longer than 90 minutes may tire the participants, while an interview of less than 30 may not be very reliable.[62] Therefore, depending on the complexity of the job, the *length* of the interview should be somewhere between 45 and 90 minutes, even if it means doing two interviews if need be.

With regard to *number*, an interview of this length allows you to ask about 10 to 20 main questions. As a reference, a question on education, training and experience, or a specific aspect of knowledge may take about two or three minutes. On the other hand, more complex questions, situational or behavioural ones for instance, can easily run to ten or twelve minutes. Each interviewer must establish his or her own yardstick.

Without specifying a number, it is obvious that several questions must be asked for each selection criterion, hence the importance of the preceding recommendation to limit the interview to a few criteria.[63] In the case of behavioural questions, we might find up to three questions for each selection criterion.

---

61. In this case, this is a content-based validation.
62. Campion *et al.* (1997).
63. Gatewood and Feild (2001).

PREPARING THE INTRODUCTION

The interview preparation is almost finished. The questions have been carefully prepared. They have been sequenced logically and appropriately for gathering the information needed. Now you have to organize the other two parts of the interview – the introduction and the conclusion. We will first turn to the introduction and its various components.

1. *Welcome.* The people who come to an interview are usually nervous. The fact that they are being evaluated by a selection committee composed of several individuals is not likely to reassure them. Thus they should get a warm welcome, to help them relax and to establish a comfortable atmosphere. Familiarity should be avoided, however: it is best to adopt a professional tone from the moment one of the committee members goes to get the candidate. The following welcoming procedure is suggested:

   a) The committee members **introduce themselves** one by one, rising, shaking the candidate's hand firmly, with genuine smiles on their faces. The interviewee must feel that he or she is important.

   b) The committee chair offers a **welcome** and **thanks** the interviewee for showing interest in the position (mentioning the name of the job specifically to avoid any confusion) and participation in the selection process.

   c) If the candidate seems particularly nervous, the committee members can take a few moments to **chat about some neutral subject**, to lower the tension, (e.g., remarks about finding a parking place, or the directions that were provided, or a positive comment about the candidate's résumé). Personal subjects should be avoided and the time for this chat limited to two or three minutes. Beating around the bush for too long may only make matters worse. The best way to make someone comfortable is to go straight to the point.

   One committee member, preferably the chair, then takes charge of providing the following information.

2. *Objectives of the interview.* Explain the objectives of the interview, which usually are: *a*) to learn about (or evaluate) the candidate's knowledge, experience and job skills in order to make a hiring decision that is both fair to the candidate and profitable for the organization, *b*) to answer the candidate's questions about the job and the organization, and *c*) to provide information on what happens next in the selection process.

3. *The committee's role.* Describe the role of the committee (e.g., making a hiring recommendation to a particular entity, as its representatives, or as outside consultants, or otherwise).

4. *Conduct of the interview.* Specify who will be asking questions, and then explain how the interview will be conducted. For example:
   - questions on education, training and experience;
   - behavioural questions ("questions asking you to provide concrete examples of things you have done and the way you work");
   - situational questions ("questions dealing with simulated situations");
   - willingness questions ("questions about your interest in this position in particular");
   - responses to the candidate's questions ("We'll take a few minutes at the end of the interview for any questions you may have").

5. *Length of the interview.* Indicate approximately how long the interview will take.

6. *Note-taking.* Point out that the committee members will be taking notes throughout the interview so that they do not forget anything when the evaluation is being done, which will enable them to treat all the candidates as fairly as possible.

7. *Signal to begin.* Ask the candidate if he or she is ready to begin. Indicate that taking some time to reflect before answering is allowable.

PREPARING THE CONCLUSION

A committee member, preferably the chair, will conclude the interview in the following manner:

1. *Termination of the interview and thanks.* Announce that the interview is over and all the questions have been asked. Thank the candidate for his or her cooperation. In a structured interview, the gathering of information should stop here. However, it is common to ask candidates if they have anything to add. (It is useful to specify the time available for this part of the interview, to avoid having candidates launch into a long story about the progress of their careers.) This additional information will be considered during the evaluation, or not, according to the interview's desired level of structure. It seems more relevant to take this information into account, since it is sometimes difficult to disregard a new factor provided by the candidate. For example, it would be hard to ignore the fact that a candidate had left a job after repeated disagreements with staff members.

2. *Summary of the job and answers to the candidate's questions.* Most people interviewed for a job have questions about the position and the organization. You should therefore respond to their expectations. It is appropriate to present a summary of the job and its various aspects, and then give the candidate an opportunity to ask a few questions. Providing this information increases a positive reaction from candidates, and helps them make an informed decision if the job is offered to them at the end of the process.

   However, the organization's representatives must carefully **plan** what information will be given and determine the time to be devoted to this.[64] They must ask themselves to what extent the interview should act as a recruitment device. (See *Step 4, Remember the Objectives of the Interview.*) The information provided must be exact and realistic.[65]

---

64. Eder and Harris (1999).
65. Breaugh (2000); Haccoun, Rigny and Bordeleau (1979).

Most specialists recommend answering the candidate's questions, but only **at the end** of the interview, after all the interviewers have asked their questions. This has several advantages, in particular:

- augmenting the standardization of the interview;
- reducing the risk of contamination by the interviewers;
- preventing the candidate from asking questions and then using the information garnered from the responses.[66]

In most cases, however, the committee has only a few minutes to devote to this step. It is not desirable to get into lengthy discussions, since many of the candidates will not be chosen. One **solution** is to ask the candidate to contact a predesignated committee member, who would be happy to respond to questions, after the interview is over. It is also possible to put all this information in a document or on a website that is accessible to the candidates.[67]

3. *End of the process.* Enumerate the other steps in the process and indicate clearly when the decision will be made and how it will be communicated. Out of respect for the candidates, and to allow them to continue their job search, if necessary, the response should be provided as quickly as possible.
4. *Departure.* End on a pleasant note ("It was nice to meet you") and say goodbye.

WRITING THE INTERVIEW GUIDE

What remains now is to put all this preparation together in a document commonly called an interview guide. This document contains at least three parts: *a*) the introduction, *b*) the prepared questions grouped in an appropriate sequence; and *c*) the conclusion. The prompting and follow-up questions are not included in the guide (except for the behavioural questions) because they must be adapted to each interviewee.[68]

66. Campion *et al.* (1997).
67. Eder and Harris (1999); Gatewood and Feild (2001).
68. Gatewood and Feild (2001); Taylor and O'Driscoll (1995).

STEP 4

CONDUCTING THE INTERVIEW

The time has come to conduct the interview and several things must be accomplished in this fourth step. (See Table 0.3, *The steps in the selection interview.*)

The importance of a professional approach. Throughout the interview, it is essential to adhere to several principles so that the approach is professional and perceived as such by the candidates. Significant advantages result from this.

a) A professional approach projects the image of a serious, well-structured organization that respects its employees, which may in return influence the candidate's decision to accept or reject the job that is offered. Even people who are turned down this time may apply for another job in the same organization if it seems solid to them. Even if they do not reapply, they can still tell other potential candidates about their positive experience.

b) A candidate is less likely to contest the resulting evaluation if the interview seems scrupulously fair. Remember that in many job competitions, the majority of people who are interviewed do not get the job, which may make them more critical.

c) In the case of litigation, a professional approach makes it easier to defend the process.

REMEMBER THE OBJECTIVES OF THE INTERVIEW

The selection interview may have various objectives, the two commonest being evaluation and recruitment. Not only can an interview serve to evaluate the candidates' skills, but it can also convince them to join the organization by describing the many advantages of the job in question. However, as in any situation, pursuing an ambiguous objective or a large number of objectives at once often leads to failure. It is best to decide whether the main objective of the interview is evaluation or recruitment.[1] If possible, it is preferable to give priority to one single objective in an interview. In the case of the interview under discussion here, we must remember that the objective is **evaluation**.

As we have mentioned previously (see the *Introduction*), the same selection process may require more than one interview. Of course, the objectives may vary depending on the interview's position in the selection process. A **preselection** interview usually aims at eliminating people who do not meet the minimum requirements, and identify and attract the most promising ones. It is not necessary to deal with all aspects, as is the case with an **in-depth** interview. If the in-depth interview takes place in two parts, you could also set aside certain aspects during the first interview and probe them more deeply during the second. Finally, the **hiring** interview, which takes place at the end of the process, is more about verifying a person's possible integration

1. Eder and Harris (1999); Gatewood and Feild (2001).

into the organization than evaluating his or her skills. Whatever the stage of the selection process, the same techniques are applied during the interview.

LIMIT ACCESS TO ANCILLARY INFORMATION

Some ancillary information about a candidate may be available prior to the interview, including: *a*) the résumé, *b*) the job application filled out by the candidate, *c*) the results he or she obtained on examinations or tests, *d*) letters of recommendation or other evidence, and *e*) the report on a previous interview.[2] Many interviewers consult this information before meeting the person in the interview. They believe this information, particularly that relating to training and experience, is essential to a good interview. Others say that these elements enable them to develop hypotheses that give direction to the interview.[3]

Problems. This practice is far from being unanimously approved by researchers, not only because the advantages have not been demonstrated, but primarily because of the problems it may cause:[4]

a) Prior checking of information may reduce the **validity** of the interview by introducing bias. Interviewers have a tendency to give much more weight to negative information, all the more if it appears early in the interview.[5] So once a candidate has been categorized, interviewers can have difficulty considering information received later.[6]

b) If the available ancillary information is not the same for all candidates, or all interviewers, or is not evaluated in the same way by all interviewers, the **reliability** (between candidates and between interviewers) will be lower.

2. Campion *et al.* (1997).
3. Gatewood and Feild (2001).
4. See Campion *et al.* (1997); Dipboye (1992); Gatewood and Feild (2001).
5. See Eder and Harris (1999).
6. See Eder and Harris (1999); Posthuma *et al.* (2002).

Ideal solutions. In theory, there are two solutions to this problem:[7]

a) The same information about the candidates is provided to all the interviewers and evaluated according to a formal, uniform procedure.

b) The information is dealt with separately, constituting another evaluation method. It is then revealed after the interview.

Other possible solutions. This second solution may seem unrealistic in contexts where it is impossible to prevent selection committee members from obtaining privileged information. Nevertheless, it is strongly recommended to consider only two kinds of ancillary information before the interview.[8] These are:

a) Information directly related to the selection criteria being evaluated in the interview. For example, if mental aptitudes are not evaluated in the interview, the results of the psychometric tests measuring these aptitudes should not be made available.

b) Incomplete or contradictory information found in the job application form or the résumé that can be clarified during the interview (e.g., a period of inactivity between two jobs, or the holding of two full-time jobs at the same time). Of course, this solution presupposes that at least one of the interviewers has analyzed all this information before the interview.

ESTABLISH FACILITATING CONDITIONS

The interview paradox and the relevance of facilitating conditions. There is a paradox inherent in the selection interview, which makes creating facilitating conditions all the more necessary. This paradox is as follow:

a) The goal of the in-depth interview is to **evaluate** candidates as objectively as possible in relation to the selection criteria.

7. Campion *et al.* (1997).
8. Gatewood and Feild (2001).

b) To do so, all the relevant **information** about the candidates must be gathered, including the more negative elements that may put them at a disadvantage. In short, you want to know the truth, the whole truth, and nothing but the (job-related) truth.

c) The candidates have all this information, but they are quite rightly interested in filtering the information so as to show themselves in the best light, in order to get the desired position. This tendency to be on the **defensive** is inherently human. It can appear in various degrees, depending on the people, in the form of a bias towards social desirability or in false answers.

d) Consequently, we must reduce the candidates' tendency to be on the defensive, or at least avoid exacerbating it, by creating appropriate **conditions** for obtaining more spontaneous and less "filtered" information.

These *facilitating* conditions may be established by adjusting the interview setting as well as the psychological atmosphere. The following are the most important of these conditions. We should make it clear, however, that establishing these conditions is less important when the interview only contains situational questions or knowledge questions.

A) Interview Setting

1. *Place.* Choose a quiet place that favours confidentiality. In order not to intimidate the candidates, especially the younger ones, try to create a comfortable ambience while maintaining the serious nature of the interview. Give the candidate a glass of water, and paper and pencil. You should also set up a place for candidates to leave their belongings.
2. *Seating the participants.* Avoid isolating the candidates; do not place them alone at the end of a big table with the committee members far away at the other end, for example. It is better to ask people to sit around a medium-sized table or side by side at a larger table. Do not make things too cramped, however, or the candidate might be able to read the interview guide, or the list of selection criteria, or the notes taken by the selection committee members.

3. *Interruptions and distractions.* Take all necessary steps to avoid being disturbed. Warn other the staff members not to come in or interrupt the interview, have telephone calls transferred, put a notice on the door, turn off all pagers and cell phones, etc.
4. *Schedule.* Set up appointments for the candidates in such a way as to have an appropriate length of time available for the interview plus some time after each to allow the committee members to finish their notes, outline an individual evaluation and take a break, if necessary. Plan for some extra time in case an interview takes longer than expected. Do not overestimate your ability to concentrate. Five or six interviews are plenty for one day.

B) Atmosphere

1. *Make sure the atmosphere favours the candidate's well-being.* Ensure that the candidates feel as comfortable as possible. As well as welcoming them, (see *Step 3, Preparing the Introduction*), you should smile, be pleasant and polite, serious without seeming solemn, use an appropriate level of language and above all, act naturally. Avoid making the situation more stressful than it already is.

   Some say that putting a little pressure on candidates during the interview makes it possible to evaluate their ability to react in a tense situation. This approach is not recommended. For one thing, candidates may react negatively. They may think that the approach is unprofessional, which may cause the kind of problems we have already discussed. (See *The importance of a professional approach.*) Second, the interviewee's entire performance may be affected by his or her ability to react to pressure. Since it is a rare job that requires people to work under pressure constantly, and the pressure felt during the interview is not necessarily the same kind as the pressure experienced in the job, this approach may harm the validity of the evaluation of the other selection criteria. When the ability to work under pressure is a job requirement, it is preferable to make this into a selection criterion that will undoubtedly be better evaluated by a simulation exercise or a work sample.

2. *Show interest in the candidate.* Show interest in and be attentive to the candidates by looking at them and reacting nonverbally to their remarks. Do not let yourself be distracted by ambient noise or what is happening outside. Candidates must feel that they are important and the interviewer is professional and trustworthy. Only under these conditions will they be willing to open up more freely.[9]

3. *Keep your opinions to yourself.* Never display your judgments or opinions, or let them show through. Expressing surprise, indicating agreement or disagreement, whether verbally or not, openly criticizing or judging a candidate negatively, all these put candidates on the defensive and cause them to mask relevant information. In the same way, discussing the candidates' remarks or simply expressing opinions can give candidates an indication of the expected responses. You have to be attentive and friendly without revealing your thoughts. However, this principle must sometimes be applied with flexibility when it is a question of preserving a candidate's self-esteem. (See *Techniques for Preserving the Candidate's Self-esteem.*)

4. *Take continuous notes.* To avoid influencing candidates' remarks, note taking by the interviewer during the interview should not give candidates any indication of the responses that are being sought. For example, taking more notes when candidates are talking about a conflict with a superior would allow them to perceive the interest taken in this kind of information and make them more suspicious for the rest of the interview. Conversely, less intense note taking may be perceived as a lack of interest. While a candidate is talking about a particularly delicate subject, some interviewers prefer to wait, out of respect, and make a note of this information a few moments later.[10] This practice is not recommended, however, because of the problems that may arise: the interviewer *a*) may forget important facts, and *b*) may be less attentive during subsequent questions.

9. Canada Revenue Agency (1992).
10. Byham (1987).

TECHNIQUES FOR MAINTAINING THE STRUCTURE AND KEEPING CONTROL OF THE INTERVIEW

You have chosen the structured job-related interview. Two levels of structure have been established as desirable in terms of the way questions are asked and sequenced. This means level 3 structure, or slightly below level 4, with prompting questions allowed so candidates can show themselves to best advantage. (See *Step 3, Standardizing the Questions and Their Sequence.*)

We will therefore consider these two ways of asking questions. The first gives the interviewer the opportunity to adapt the questions to the candidate's responses, which is less possible with the second, more standardized, more rigid method. Professionals, even the strictest ones, tend to show a little flexibility, although certain purists prefer to follow the order of questions set out in the interview guide.[11]

While the interview is going on, the interviewer has several ways of maintaining control and following the prepared interview guide (*Step 3*).[12] These include the following:

1. *Avoiding digressions and useless details.* To interrupt candidates politely when they digress or give details that are not relevant, the interviewer may:

   a) Inform the person that the selection committee **does not have the time necessary** to cover all aspects of his or her experience (e.g., "That's interesting, but at this stage of the process, we must stick to the essential aspects of your job experience" or "If we have the time, we'll come back to that later").

   b) **Redirect** the conversation (e.g., "It's very interesting that you computerized the planning and monitoring of the international projects. But earlier you mentioned that you were responsible for negotiating the contracts with various departments. Could you tell me whether...").

11. Byham (1987); Campion *et al.* (1997); Gatewood and Feild (2001); Taylor and O'Driscoll (1995).
12. Byham (1987); Canada Revenue Agency (1992); Taylor and O'Driscoll (1995).

2. *Not accepting vague or incomplete answers.* When a candidate gives a vague or incomplete answer, the interviewer can:

   a) Ask the candidate to **clarify** the response (e.g., "So you were the one who made the decision. I'd like you to give me more details on the way that decision was made, the criteria that were considered, who was concerned, etc.").

   b) Clarify the question by **rephrasing** it (e.g., "What I meant was, how do you make the decision to stop a project in the planning stages? Every organization has its own procedures. How does it work at your company?").

3. *Making the candidate responsible.* One way of maintaining the interview structure is to make the candidate responsible for the conduct of the interview and keeping to the schedule. To accomplish this, the interviewer can use one or other of the two following methods:[13]

   a) A half an hour before the interview, the candidate can be provided with the list of questions. Set up in an adjoining room, he or she will have the opportunity to prepare by making notes and thinking about possible responses. During the interview, the candidate can refer to the questions as well as the notes made during the preparation period. This method lessens the candidate's concerns about the questions that will be asked and reduces hesitations when responding. Giving candidates a moment to think also reduces the likelihood of vague and incomplete responses.

   b) At the start of the interview, the interviewer can give the candidate written or verbal instructions that he or she is responsible for managing the time. For example, the interviewer might say, "You have 60 minutes to answer the 8 questions you were given at the beginning of the interview. We're leaving it up to you to devote the amount of time you think is appropriate to each question." Of course, the interviewer must make sure that the candidate has a watch or that there is a clock on the wall. Experience has shown that the great majority of candidates stay within the established parameters.

---

13. It should be noted, however, that these methods are not widely used.

TECHNIQUES FOR PRESERVING THE CANDIDATE'S SELF-ESTEEM

All interviewers who call themselves professionals have an obligation to preserve the candidate's confidence and self-esteem. In addition to all the previously mentioned reasons (see *The importance of a professional approach* and *The interview paradox and the relevance of facilitating conditions*), this essentially involves showing the most basic respect. The following techniques will maintain the candidate's self-esteem during the interview:[14]

1. *Empathy.* Show empathy and understanding when a person gives negative information for which is not easy to find a justification (e.g., nod, smile, say something like, "I understand. That must have been very frustrating. The situation was not easy.").
2. *Gentle insistence.* Show sympathy as well as perseverance when a person is clearly trying to avoid answering a question. Politely insist, and keep trying without being aggressive (e.g., "I understand that it is not always easy to find an example, but what interests me is a situation in which...").[15] Avoid forcing a person to openly admit a mistake. The interviewer who does not obtain a response after several attempts should move on to the next subject (e.g., "OK, I see. If you don't mind, we can come back to that question a little later. Now, can you give an example..."). The same kind of remarks can be used for silences, or when the candidate is visibly unable to respond. However, the subject should not be changed too quickly, for as we know, a little pressure may cause the candidate to disclose important facts. When a question remains unanswered, it may be useful to come back to it towards the end of the interview (e.g., "Before we finish, let's go back to the question... Remember? We asked you to give us an example of..."). Again, it is better not to insist if the person continues to be unable to respond.

---

14. Byham (1987); Eder and Harris (1999); Canada Revenue Agency (1992).
15. Canada Revenue Agency (1992).

3. *Prior justification.* When asking a question that will probably provoke some negative information, offer the candidate some prior justification (e.g., "Everybody makes mistakes every once in a while...").

4. *Sincere compliments.* Compliment candidates on past achievements (e.g., "That's quite an increase in sales volume. Very impressive!"), or on their performance in the interview (e.g., "You are very methodical in your answers. That makes it very easy to follow."). These compliments must be sincere, or the interviewer will achieve exactly the opposite effect – the candidate may react negatively. In addition, the compliments must not reveal aspects of the expected responses. This is a major risk that must be seriously considered. In the case of a highly structured interview, this technique should be avoided.

Appendix H contains an exercise on techniques to maintain the interview's structure and preserve the candidate's self-esteem.

LET THEM TALK: YOU LISTEN

Remember that the objective of the interview is to evaluate the candidate by collecting the information needed for this evaluation. Therefore, you have to let the candidate **talk** and you have to know how to listen. In fact, the person being interviewed should be talking the most, up to 80% of the interview time according to the 80/20 rule (80% of the time allotted to the candidate and 20% to the interviewer). Encourage the candidate with pauses, nods, or other indications, to avoid losing precious minutes of information-collecting time.

Knowing how to keep quiet is not necessarily the same thing as knowing how to **listen**. A number of interviewers, especially those just beginning, find it hard to listen when they are thinking about the next question they have to ask. For this reason, a complete interview guide can be an invaluable aid for the interviewer who must concentrate on the interviewee's responses and try to fully understand their meaning.

OBSERVE CERTAIN RULES OF CONDUCT

The interviewer and the selection committee members must observe the following rules during the interview:

1. *Make yourself understood.* Take the necessary steps to ensure that the interviewee understands the questions (e.g., by asking clear questions and rephrasing the question if necessary).
2. *Make sure you understand.* Try to understand what the interviewee is saying or indicating (e.g., with the help of prompting questions or, sometimes, the restatement technique).
3. *Do not evaluate prematurely.* Some interviewers have a tendency to evaluate candidates from the moment they walk into the interview room, which can keep them from considering all the information gathered afterwards, particularly information that contradicts their premature evaluation. The best way of neutralizing this tendency is to follow the interview guide that was prepared and make notes on nothing but facts and observations.
4. *Do not try to confirm your opinions.* In order to verify your first impressions or hypotheses, you, the interviewer, should reconcile them with the new information resulting from the interview.[16] You should actively look for facts that contradict these opinions, in particular with behavioural questions dealing with counter-examples. Following the interview guide closely and taking proper notes are also good ways of fighting this tendency.
5. *Verify information.* Cultivate skepticism and constantly try to verify information by asking additional questions if necessary.[17]
6. *Do not talk between interviews.* When the formal evaluation of the candidate does not take place immediately after the interview, it is best not to discuss the candidates and their responses with the other interviewers, in order to maintain uniformity of procedure and evaluation standards.[18] If there has to be some kind of informal exchange after each interview, a common practice, you

16. Posthuma *et al.* (2002).
17. Eder and Harris (1999).
18. Campion *et al.* (1997).

should at least avoid making any overall judgments like, "She was really good," or, "I think that was the worst candidate we've seen." This kind of remark can bias the judgment of the other selection committee members.

TAKING NOTES

Advantages. During the interview, the interviewers must take notes in order to:[19]

- monitor the way the interview is going, to make sure that the necessary information is being obtained (e.g., a complete description of a behaviour after a behavioural question);
- allow those who are listening to pay closer attention;
- indicate to the candidate the seriousness of the approach and establish the good reputation of the organization;
- provide a clear and exhaustive report of the information obtained, which will be used for *a*) evaluation, *b*) decision-making, and *c*) discussions with the other selection committee members, or for providing appropriate justification *d*) if the candidate asks questions, *e*) for a report to the organization, or *f*) in case of an appeal or litigation;
- help integrate all the information;
- avoid resorting to a general impression and limit biases.

Disadvantages. Unfortunately, note taking may have some disadvantages. It may:[20]

- tell the candidate what information is being sought and will be used in making the decision;
- be disconcerting for the candidate if the interviewer overdoes it and only looks at his or her notes.

19. Burnett *et al.* (1998); Byham (1987); Campion *et al.* (1997).
20. Burnett *et al.* (1998); Eder and Harris (1999).

Solutions. We have already explained how to get around the first disadvantage by taking notes continuously (see *Atmosphere*). The interviewer can avoid the second disadvantage by using the following methods:

- only noting the main or **important points**;
- sharing the tasks among **several interviewers** (one asks the questions while the others take notes);
- establishing an atmosphere of trust and showing interest in other ways (e.g., agreeing with the candidate, intermittent visual contact, etc.).

Audio- or videotaping is very rarely used. In addition to the technical problems which can always occur, the interviewer must listen to the interview a second time to get all the relevant information, which requires a great deal of time.[21] Some critics point out that interviewees almost always react negatively, but others have suggested that in fact, the selection committee members are the ones opposed to this practice, which obliges them to behave professionally and follow the interview protocol faithfully.

The effect on validity. Note taking during the interview has no marked or systematic effect on the validity of the results.[22] Other elements seem to factor in.[23] For example, when note taking is done on a **voluntary** basis, those who take notes generally obtain a higher level of validity than the others. The validity also increases when the **content** of the notes deals with the actions reported by the candidate (e.g., "Corrected the mistake," "Went voluntarily," or "Takes responsibility"), whether the note taking was voluntary or mandatory. On the other hand, it may be that certain kinds of notes decrease the validity, such as noting the behaviour that the candidate exhibits during the interview (e.g., "Speaks softly," "Doesn't answer," "Looks in the eyes"). However, the advantages of note taking are in no way diminished by these ambivalent results with regard to validity.

21. Byham (1987).
22. Huffcutt and Woehr (1999).
23. Burnett *et al.* (1998).

A) What to Note

Facts and observations. Notes must primarily deal with facts and observations, such as in:

- **verbatim** reports of the interviewee's responses, dropping the unnecessary words to speed up the note taking process (e.g., "Degree in chemistry, 3.8 average out of 4.3," "consulted my colleagues even if they were not in agreement...," "my boss gave me the job of setting up...");
- **behaviour** observed during the interview that relates to the chosen selection criteria (e.g., "Does not answer the question," "Doesn't finish the answer," "Long silence").

What to avoid. Everything **irrelevant** must be excluded, everything that has no relationship to the selection criteria to be measured or the job in question. However, what should be done with information that is not related to the selection criteria, but which is relevant to the job? For example, suppose that the list of criteria does not include honesty, yet the selection committee members note several times during the interview that the candidate is not telling the truth. First of all, you have to remember a fundamental principle. In a selection context, and this principle is well explained in the *Standards for Educational and Psychological Testing* (AERA, APA and NCME, 1999), validity must be established not in relation to the selection criteria, but in relation to the job, or more precisely to behaviours or the results produced by these behaviours. The fundamental consequence of this principle is that the selection criteria are subordinate to the job, and not the other way around. For example, in case of an error or omission in determining the selection criteria, the job takes precedence. Consequently, if the job requires honesty, you have to consider the fact that a person lies as relevant information, even if that is not stated in the selection criteria. Is that a breach of the standardization process? Probably. But still, standardization is a means, not an end in itself, since the goal is validity (i.e., the ability to predict on-the-job behaviour). Nevertheless, if an action is brought before a tribunal, will the judge see it the same way? That depends on the judge, the explanations he or she is given and the judge's understanding of the situation. After all, the judge is not an expert in selection.

It is equally important to avoid **interpretations** and judgments (e.g., *does not want* to answer the question, shows a *superficial* interest in the job, *lack of leadership*). Notes may contain a few interpretations and judgments, if absolutely necessary, as long as *a*) they are obvious inferences, *b*) they are considered as hypotheses to be verified later, or *c*) the interviewers are able to see the difference between an interpretation and an observation.[24] Appendix I includes an exercise on distinguishing between a fact and an observation.

You must also avoid **evaluating** (scoring) the responses during the interview, even if you are have situational questions with a scoring guide.[25] At this stage, you must confine yourself to noting responses and observations, because notes composed of evaluations, interpretations or judgments do not allow interviewers to reconsider their opinions later, or discuss the candidate objectively with the selection committee, or write a report about the information received for feedback or litigation purposes.

B) When to Take Notes

Notes must be taken **during** the interview and if necessary completed **immediately afterwards.**[26] The longer the interviewer waits before getting it down on paper, the greater the risk of forgetting facts and only retaining a general impression.[27] If the interview guide or the evaluation sheet requires that the selection committee members check off correct answers, it must be done discretely.

---

24. In certain circumstances, where labour relations are particularly contentious and the probability of litigation higher, it is best to avoid making note of interpretations and judgments. The employer may be called to produce in court the notes that were taken during an interview and defend their propriety. If the notes contain interpretations and judgments, it may be more difficult for the employer to justify them. The following is an exceptional but real example. During a job competition in the public service, the interviewer noted, "The candidate is ill at ease and does not like to interact with others." The candidate, a native of another country, took the case before a tribunal and brought in an expert on intercultural differences. It was an interesting debate, but one that could have been avoided if the interviewer had not written down this judgment.
25. Taylor and O'Driscoll (1995).
26. Taylor and O'Driscoll (1995).
27. Byham (1987).

C) How to Take Notes

Note taking can be organized in various ways.

1. *On blank sheets of paper.* The interviewer takes notes on blank sheets of paper as the interview unfolds. It is useful to establish a few conventions, such as indicating the question number (e.g., Q3a) and whether the notes are verbatim (e.g., using quotation marks), an observation (e.g., by enclosing the observation in square brackets) or an interpretation (e.g., placing an I before the note).

   Many professional interviewers prefer to use blank sheets. They allow greater flexibility, but also take more effort. To take note of relevant information, the interviewer and the selection committee members must have the responses defined by the list of selection criteria and their indicators in mind (or before their eyes), and at the same time follow the interview guide containing the questions. In addition, when the interview is over, the information collected must be reorganized and rewritten, usually under each of the selection criteria, in order to be able to evaluate the candidate criterion by criterion (e.g., rewrite and group together all the information about the criterion "Ability to lead", or "Negotiating skills," etc.) The reorganization will be greatly facilitated with an evaluation sheet such as the one presented in Table 4.1. In practice, only the most meticulous interviewers do this reorganization; others, constrained by time or other demands, only reorganize this information in their minds, without rewriting it according to criteria.

2. *Interview guide.* Interviewers can write their notes directly in an interview guide that has a space for notes under each question. In this case, each interviewer must have an interview guide for each candidate (e.g., 5 candidates × 3 interviewers = 15 guides). Furthermore, the sequence of questions need not follow the order of selection criteria chosen for the interview.

   It is relatively simple to write notes directly in the guide; in fact, it is a more secure method for less experienced interviewers. They only have to note the candidate's responses and their own observations as the questions are asked. However, should a response contain information that is unexpected in terms of the question

TABLE 4.1

Example of an evaluation sheet for selecting a candidate for professor

Candidate: ____________________ Date of preselection: ____________________

Discipline: ____________________ Date of 1st interview: ____________________

Date of 2nd interview: ____________________

Reference checks: ____________________

Based on the résumé, interviews and other selection tools, fill out the following rubric, then evaluate each criterion with the following rating scale:

Unsuitable	Weak	Good	Very good	Excellent
1	2	3	4	5

Evaluation ☐

1. **Ability to teach** (Teaching methods, communication)

Criterion	Interviewer's notes	
Training in teaching skills (Course, seminars, readings, etc.)	*None.* *A few conferences and reading some pedagogical papers from the university's teaching support service*	+
Knowledge about teaching methods (taxonomy of educational objectives, adequacy of objectives-means-evaluation, etc.)	*Knows Bloom's taxonomy*	+
Courses given, number of times, level, group size, etc.	*Undergrad HRM, 3 times, 20 - 40/class* *Research methods, once, MBA, class of 12*	+
Teaching evaluations obtained from the students	*Yes, between 3.2 and 3.5 out of 4.0*	+
Students' perception of the candidate and his or her teaching	*Prepared, marks carefully* *Nervous, not fully in charge of the class*	±
Teaching methods used, past and future	*Past: Presentations, case studies* *Wants to do role playing*	+
Interest in teaching - Level - Area - Importance in relation to other academic duties	*– Undergraduate and master's* *– HRM, methodology, OB* *Research > teaching > administrative duties*	+
Expresses him- or herself clearly and concisely	*Very clear, sometimes long-winded, with a lot of details*	±
Logical, structured, easy to follow	*(VG) "First, second, etc."*	+
Grabs attention, stimulating	*Monotone, doesn't gesticulate, serious, no humour (seems tense)*	–
Other indicators and observations	*Freelance management training, for a consulting firm, 2 years, 2 to 4 days a month*	

The full evaluation sheet in its actual format includes five selection criteria. The words in script type are the interviewer's notes.

that has just been asked, but expected for another question in the guide, the interviewer must include a reference to the appropriate question. In addition, if the candidates are being evaluated by criteria, as with blank sheets of paper, the information must be reorganized and rewritten under each of the criteria, once the interview is over.

3. *Interview guide in which the questions are organized by selection criteria.* Here the notes are written in the interview guide, but this time, the questions are grouped according to selection criteria (e.g., questions on the ability to lead, questions on negotiating skills, etc.) Table 4.2 presents an excerpt of an interview guide composed of behavioural questions that integrates note taking at the same time.

   Using an interview guide in which the questions are organized according to selection criteria eliminates the final difficulty noted for the preceding organization method. However attractive this approach seems, it has one important limitation: it only facilitates note-taking when each question deals with a single selection criterion. If the interviewer wants to use questions whose responses include information concerning several selection criteria at once, he or she will once again face the problem of organizing the information as it is received. That is why some professionals still prefer to write everything down on their trusty notepad and then, after the interview, reorganize everything according to criteria.

4. *Evaluation sheet.* The interviewer makes notes in the space provided on the evaluation sheet (or scoring guide) containing the selection criteria chosen for the interview and their indicators (or the expected responses). Table 4.1 shows an example of an evaluation sheet filled out by an interviewer.

   Writing notes on the evaluation sheet during the interview avoids having to reorganize the information. However, unless the questions are in the same order as the selection criteria appear on the sheet, it will be difficult to fill in the information as it is obtained under the corresponding selection criterion. In fact, this approach is convenient only if *a*) the sheet has few criteria to evaluate and

TABLE 4.2

Excerpt from an interview guide with questions grouped by selection criteria

Leadership: Ability to use appropriate methods to direct and influence the way a person or a group of people carry out activities so that established objectives are achieved

Examples of indicators:

- Gains the attention, respect and trust of others
- Gets a person or a group to subscribe to an idea or a way of proceeding
- Influences the positions taken by those in authority to obtain desired results
- Becomes accepted and takes leadership of the group
- Motivates personnel effectively to achieve desired objectives.

Question 1: Give an example that took place within the last few months of an instance in which your employees succeeded in getting you to change a decision.

- Situation:
- Actions:
- Results:

Question 2: It sometimes happens that we need the help of people who are not under our authority. Can you give an example where you had to obtain the cooperation of a group outside your unit?

- Situation:
- Actions:
- Results:

Question 3: Tell us about a situation in which you were not able to motivate your staff effectively.

- Situation:
- Actions:
- Results:

Evaluation:

Unacceptable	Weak	Good	Very good	Excellent
1	2	3	4	5

Comments:

few indicators, and *b*) the interview is conducted by a committee, in which one person asks the questions and the others take down the information.

5. *Interview guide in which the questions are scored by a rating scale.* The notes are taken in the interview guide in which each question is accompanied by a rating scale made up of the indicators or expected responses. Table 4.3 is an example of this type,

TABLE 4.3
Example of scoring with a behaviourally anchored rating scale

Criterion evaluated: *Human resources management* Job: Head nurse	
Question: It is just before Christmas. Two nurses on your team call to tell you they will be absent as of tomorrow night, giving valid reasons. You will not have enough team members to do the job. How would you resolve this problem?	
Expected responses:	
1 point	The hospital has a pool of replacements. They should find staff to cover. *OR* There's nothing I can do about it. The private agency will take charge of finding staff. *OR* I would tell the two nurses that they have to come to work. I wouldn't give them any choice.
3 points	I would discuss the situation with my superior. I would consider the possibility of moving a few patients to another ward or I would call the agency. *OR* I would try and convince the two nurses to come to an agreement so that only one would be absent, and I would fill the missing position with help from the agency.
5 points	I would discuss the situation with my manager. I would check to see if there might be any staff available from another ward. I would contact the agency to find out what the replacement possibilities are. If these possibilities fail, I would call on part-time or casual nurses. If I couldn't find any, I would consider the possibility of moving a few patients into another unit. If nothing else worked, I would replace one of the two nurses myself.

Adapted from Taylor and O'Driscoll (1995), p. 137–8.
Note: This method requires that the three response levels be mutually exclusive.

where space was left for note-taking for each indicator, or overall, for each selection criterion. (See *Step 3*.) This way of taking notes lends itself well to situational and behavioural questions.

When each question in the interview guide is followed by expected responses or indicators, the interviewer only has to check the aspect observed or write observations relating to each. Each question may deal with more than one selection criterion as long as the expected responses for each of the criteria evaluated by this question are written down. When the interviewer has finished making notes, however, all the information obtained will have to be put together, criterion by criterion.

Consistency with the evaluation method. No matter what its advantages and disadvantages are, the way the note taking is organized must be consistent with the evaluation method chosen: by questions, by criteria, etc. (See *Step 5*.)

Mental image. To be able to remember each candidate, it is practical to take a mental photograph of them. A simple description can be enough (e.g., "the tall blond guy with the round glasses," "the woman with the curly hair and the black and white dress," etc.). This description may be useful when it is time for the evaluation, or making a decision, if you have to compare candidates or remind yourself of facts that were neglected during note taking. To avoid any problems, some interviewers prefer to indicate this information on a separate sheet and destroy it once the evaluation is over.

CONDUCTING AN INTERVIEW BY COMMITTEE

Advantages. Interviewing with a selection committee is neither new nor unusual. Even though it is more expensive, working with a committee offers the several advantages. A committee format:[28]

- ensures the participation of everyone involved in making the decision;

28. Byham (1987); Campion *et al.* (1997); Dipboye (1992); Eder and Harris (1999); Taylor and O'Driscoll (1995).

- provides common evaluation conditions for each member of the committee;
- calls on experts for each aspect evaluated;
- encourages members to be more structured;
- allows one interviewer to ask questions while the others take notes;
- reduces bias and omissions, inappropriate inferences and other errors by combining the perceptions of several people;
- gives interviewers more confidence in their decisions;
- increases the acceptance of decisions by candidates and the organization;
- makes the decision easier to defend in case of litigation.

Effect on validity. Despite the many presumed advantages in reducing evaluation errors, the results of studies comparing the validity of interviews conducted by a single interviewer with that of interviews conducted by a committee are ambiguous. The effect on validity is not systematic: sometimes there is an increase, sometimes not, and in rare cases, a decrease.[29] For example, although using a committee in a low-structure interview seems to make the interview more valid than using a single interviewer, there is almost no difference when the interview is structured.

Number of committee members. The number of people in a selection committee should not be too large, for fear of intimidating the interviewees, nor too small, so the advantages mentioned above are not lost. In most cases, three to five people are adequate for an effective committee – a 10-member committee seems excessive.[30]

29. Eder and Harris (1999); Huffcutt and Woehr (1999).
30. See Campion *et al.* (1997).

Factors to consider in choosing committee members. Choosing members of a selection committee is a critical task. The following factors should be considered:[31]

- knowledge and skills in relation to the job under consideration;
- availability and inclination to act as committee member;
- impartiality;
- competence in selection interviewing;
- status, category and level of the person's job in relation to that of the job to be filled.

Assign roles and set the operating procedures. Working in committee requires that you clarify roles and establish operating procedures to be maintained throughout the process. For example, you must decide who will welcome the candidate, who will outline the interview procedure, who will ask which questions, who will terminate the interview. You must also decide who will intervene and at what time. Interviewers must be reminded of the various techniques to be used and the rules of conduct that should be observed in the interview. The following scenarios offer two interesting illustrations.

a) The **first** scenario is to have the most senior person or the person who represents authority welcome the candidate, give the introduction and terminate the interview. Then the human resources representative, or the person who is most qualified to do the interviewing, is given the job of asking all the prepared questions in the interview guide. The other committee members can intervene at any time to obtain clarification, but they should signal their intervention to the main interviewer, so as not to interrupt the questioning. At the end of each group of questions (determined in advance), they can also ask prompting or follow-up questions.

This scenario has two **advantages**. First, the committee members, with the exception of the interviewer, can concentrate on the candidate and take notes at their leisure. Second, the candidate

31. Adapted from Secrétariat du Conseil du trésor (2001), *Module 9*.

cannot falsely accuse any member of the committee of having treated him or her unfairly by asking an inappropriate question. However, this scenario may create a psychological distance between the committee members and the candidate and therefore be intimidating.

b) In the **second** scenario, the questions are divided about equally between the committee members. The introduction and conclusion may be left to the person who represents authority and the interviewers then ask their questions in turn. As in the first scenario, the other interviewers may ask prompting questions. In addition, the person asking the questions commonly does not take notes at the same time, in order to maintain visual contact with the candidate. The other members of the committee take on this responsibility. It is usually understood that the committee members ask the same question each time to all the candidates in order to maintain a high level of standardization.

This scenario also has two **advantages**. First, the active participation of all members of the committee helps create a dynamic atmosphere that seems more like a conversation than an evaluation by a jury. Second, it allows each member of the committee to have personal contact with the candidate.

USING THE SAME INTERVIEWERS FOR ALL CANDIDATES

The interviews for all candidates must be conducted by the same interviewers, particularly if they are not very structured. The reasons for this are twofold. **First**, if the interviewers do not ask all the same questions or if they evaluate each of the answers in the their own way, or are not even the same people, how can you tell if the differences in evaluation come from the candidates' performances or variable behaviour on the part of the interviewers?[32] **Second**, interviewers are not all equally skilled and the validity of their interviews may vary,

32. Campion *et al.* (1997); Huffcutt and Woehr (1999).

especially when the interviews are less structured.[33] Therefore, the same interviewers must be used to maintain consistency between interviews.

Compromise solutions. It is sometimes difficult, even impossible, to use the same interviewers when, for example, a very large number of candidates need to be interviewed in a short time or when the interviews take place in locations spread over a large territory. Compromise solutions must then be considered. The following are possible solutions.

a) Entrust the handling of all the interviews to one or two interviewers.[34]

b) Use selection committees composed of different members, but stick to a highly standardized strategy. To do so, several steps may be taken:
   - Each committee member is completely trained (usually a day-long training session) on the format and content of the interview, how to take notes, etc.
   - Strict rules are established about the way the interviews are conducted (e.g., duration, introduction, order of the questions, etc.).
   - A detailed and explicit evaluation sheet is used by all committees.
   - Each committee includes at least one manager who knows the job and a human resources specialist who is experienced in selection interviews.
   - The committee members communicate with each other on regular basis, particularly to standardize the interpretation and evaluation of the candidates' responses, discuss difficulties encountered and agree on solutions.
   - If necessary, descriptive statistics (e.g., mean and standard deviation) of the evaluations done by each committee are calculated during the process. If there are significant differences, it is important to find the cause and take the appropriate steps

33. See Campion *et al.* (1997); Dipboye (1992); Eder and Harris (1989); Posthuma *et al.* (2002).
34. Campion *et al.* (1997).

to rectify the situation. However, statistics must be used with extreme caution. A difference in the mean between two committees may simply reflect an actual difference between the two samples of candidates. Conversely, the fact that two committees have similar means for their evaluations does not necessarily mean that their evaluations are comparable. For that to be true, the two groups of candidates would have to be equivalent.

- An independent evaluator rereads the interview notes taken by the members of the different committees and compares their evaluations. Any inconsistency should be discussed during the regular communication between committees. However, this way of doing things can be very complicated in practice.

Obviously, applying all these measures requires a great deal of effort on the part of the organization, the committee members in particular. Their relevance must be determined on a case by case basis, remembering that standardization, as a general rule, is an important condition for ensuring validity and fairness in the personnel selection process.

STEP 5

EVALUATION

The interview has enabled you to gather all the candidate's information for each of the selection criteria. Now that information must be evaluated to decide whether the candidate is qualified for the job (see Table 0.3, *The steps in the selection interview*). How do you go about it?

STANDARDIZING THE EVALUATION

Three levels of structure or standardization may be used to evaluate the interviewees.[1]

1. Campion *et al.* (1997); Huffcutt and Arthur (1994).

Level 1 Low structure: **Overall** evaluation at the end of the interview.

Level 2 High structure: Evaluation of **each selection criterion** at the end of the interview based on *a*) the responses to a group of questions organized by criteria, or *b*) the entire interview.

Level 3 Maximum structure: Evaluation of **each question** during or at the end of the interview, using a guide containing the responses expected for each of the questions.

The structured job-related interview requires a standardized evaluation. In terms of **reliability**, level 3 seems to be the best.[2] It is certainly less complex for evaluators to assess the answer to each question than to evaluate all the answers to several questions or the entire interview. However, in terms of **validity**, the superiority of level 3 over level 2 has not been conclusively demonstrated.[3] Pending evidence to the contrary, **levels 2 and 3** can therefore be **recommended.**[4]

It goes without saying that the evaluation system chosen will be the **same** for all the candidates and will be scrupulously applied in the same way. In addition, **after each interview**, the interviewer must do the evaluation alone, without talking to any of the other interviewers, but also review these evaluations periodically, either after a certain number of analyses of the results or after a given time period.[5]

EVALUATION BY QUESTIONS

Evaluating by questions consists of evaluating the responses that the candidate provided for each question. To do this, the interviewers use a guide containing the expected response components. As with the situational questions in *Step 3*, the evaluation can be done by *a*) simply adding up the points for each response, or *b*) evaluating the response overall by referring to a behaviourally anchored rating scale (see Tables 3.2 and 3.3).

---

2. See Campion *et al.* (1997); Eder and Harris (1999).
3. See Eder and Harris (1999); Huffcutt and Arthur (1994).
4. Catano *et al.* (1997); Dipboye (1992); Taylor and O'Driscoll (1995).
5. Taylor and O'Driscoll (1995).

In addition to its use with situational questions, evaluation by questions is also easily applied to knowledge and behavioural questions that are accompanied by a correction guide organized by question. However, it is less effective for other kinds of questions for which there are no actual objective answer sheets.

EVALUATION BY CRITERIA

Evaluation by selection criteria is probably the most widespread. The interviewees' responses are grouped by selection criteria, then evaluated with predetermined indicators for each criterion (See *Step 2, Determining the Indicators or Expected Responses*.) This is therefore a two-step process: classification of the information obtained, followed by its evaluation. Evaluation by criteria is applicable to all types of questions.

A) Classifying the Information Obtained

Having gathered the candidate's information, the interviewer must organize it according to each selection criterion chosen for the interview. This step basically consists in **content analysis**.

In certain cases, the questions from the interview guide are grouped by criteria, whereas in others they are organized differently, chronologically, for example. (See *Step 3, Preparing and Sequencing the Questions*.)

Questions organized by criteria. We have already presented an example of the kind of interview guide that integrates evaluation with note-taking. (See Table 4.2.) Most of the candidate's responses to the three questions presented in this table provide several pieces of information that are relevant to the criterion being evaluated – leadership. It may be, however, that some information will be found elsewhere: a) in one of the responses to interview questions related to other criteria, b) in one of the responses to general questions about experience, or c) outside of the interview itself, in another source of information (e.g., the résumé). Sometimes a question will produce information related to more than one selection criterion or with another criterion than the one expected. Therefore this information must be correctly classified under each of the relevant selection criteria. To do so, the interviewer must carefully examine all the information obtained and make sure it is appropriately classified under each criterion.

Questions not organized by criteria. Since no item of information is classified in advance, an evaluation sheet can be very useful. The evaluation sheet is a separate document that is not integrated with the interview guide. It can take various forms. The most widely used format usually includes a definition of each selection criterion and its indicators (see Table 2.3, *Example of a selection criterion definition and its indicators*, and Table 4.1, *Example of an evaluation sheet for the selection of a candidate for professor*). As for notes, they can be written in the interview guide, on blank sheets or on the evaluation sheet. (See *Step 4, Taking Notes.*) Appendix J presents an exercise on classifying responses based on the selection criteria.

B) Evaluating the Information

Having properly classified the information obtained, you must evaluate the candidate on each criterion, referring to their specific indicators. To accomplish this, we suggest a *three-phase approach* that presupposes dealing with one criterion at a time.[6]

Phase 1: Examining all the information classified under the same criterion. You must begin by carefully examining all the information that has been classified under one criterion in order to develop a valid understanding. It may also be useful to add comments about the information, perhaps in the margins or on a different worksheet, making sure you number the items of information.[7] For example, the

6. Byham (1987).
7. When the evaluation is done in a context where the risks of a legal challenge are sizeable, it would be wise to write comments on a separate worksheet that will be destroyed once the evaluation is done. These comments are only a temporary, informal work tool, and only the final evaluation of each criterion, with its appropriate justification, has any real importance.

evaluator may indicate with a [+] or [–] if the information is positive or negative, or a [*] if it is important, or an [R] if the experience was recent.

Phase 2: Weighing the information and considering the way its elements interact. The evaluation of a selection criterion cannot be limited to a simple mechanical compilation like a sum or an average of the score assigned to each item of information. **First,** not every piece of information has the same importance in relation to the criterion being evaluated. For example, an isolated instance of a behaviour going back to the beginning of the candidate's career does not have the same weight as five years of successful experience in a job identical to the one being offered. So the scope of the achievement, its recent nature and its relevance to the job are all factors that affect the weight to be given to the information. **Second,** the relationships between the various items of information and the way they fit together are in themselves significant. (For example, in all the cases where a particular candidate had failed, it was for a project in which the team was made up of sub-contractors.) In this regard, a progression in experience or improvements in achievement are significant factors.

Phase 3: Evaluating. All that remains to do is to evaluate all the items of information by assigning a score for each criterion. This is done with an appropriate scale (various examples are presented below, under *Recommended Rating Scales*). In spite of all the refinements that are made when creating a rating scale, evaluation always requires some judgment.

BY QUESTIONS OR BY CRITERIA?

Both approaches to evaluation, using questions or criteria, are appropriate when they are rigorously done, i.e., following the recommendations and techniques described above. However, to help you choose, it may be useful to compare the two approaches.

Advantages and Disadvantages of the Two Approaches

1. *Validity.* We have already mentioned that the validity of evaluation by questions over that by criteria has not been demonstrated conclusively.

2. *Reliability.* Evaluation by questions, because of its greater standardization, ensures a higher reliability.[8]

3. *Compliance with the law and the organization's policies, as well as legal defensibility.* Evaluation by questions is intrinsically more mechanical, and therefore more objective. It should be easier to defend in case of a dispute or legal challenge.[9]

4. *Ease of preparation.* With the approach by questions, the preparation of a correction guide requires a great deal of work, because all the expected responses must be planned for, as far as possible. In addition, the response components are question- and job-specific, which means starting all over again for each new case or context. With evaluation by criteria, the indicators are more generic and therefore easier to adapt from one job to another.

5. *Ease of application.* The approach by questions is much less complex for evaluators than the approach by criteria, which requires judgment and interpretation.

6. *Flexibility.* The approach by questions is mechanical and rigid. When the evaluation guide has been prepared, there is little opportunity to adapt it to the candidates' peculiarities. The approach by criteria, on the other hand, is more flexible, because of its generic indicators.[10]

Table 5.1 summarizes the advantages and disadvantages of the two approaches.

---

8. See Campion *et al.* (1997); Eder and Harris (1999).
9. See Pettersen (2000) on the advantages of mechanical correction.
10. Pettersen (2000).

TABLE 5.1
Advantages (+) and disadvantages (–) of evaluating by questions and by criteria

	Evaluation by questions	Evaluation by criteria
1. Validity	++	++
2. Reliability	++	+
3. Compliance with the law and legal defensibility	++	+
4. Ease of preparation	– –	–
5. Ease of application	++	+
6. Flexibility	–	++

Evaluating by questions then by criteria. It is possible to proceed with an evaluation by criteria after having done an evaluation by questions. This is a matter of taking the total (or the mean) of the questions for each criterion. In this case, the questions must deal with a single selection criterion at a time.

RECOMMENDED RATING SCALES

Gradations and descriptors. Except for the case in which the evaluation is done by questions and by totalling the points assigned for each the expected responses, a rating scale is needed to standardize the evaluations among candidates and among interviewers. The reader will find an example of a rating scale in the *Evaluation sheet for selecting a candidate for professor* (Table 4.1). This scale includes five gradations for which the descriptors are adjectives. Other examples are included in Appendix E.

Types of rating scales. Many scales have been proposed over the years, each designed according to a methodology that was intended to ensure maximum objectivity.[11] It is possible to organize these scales into four main types, according to the descriptors used as anchors for each of the gradations (see Table 5.2).[12]

11. See Guion (1998).
12. Campion *et al.* (1997).

TABLE 5.2

Four types of rating scales classified according to the descriptors used as anchors

Anchors	Type 1: Expected responses	Type 2: Definition or generic indicators	Type 3: Adjectives	Type 4: Comparisons
5 points	Organizes tasks in several categories according to a system that he or she has established.	Uses a system to index the tasks and establish priorities.	Excellent	Top 20%
4 points	Sees what is necessary and then prepares a program for accomplishing it.		Very good	Next 20%
3 points		Evaluates the importance of tasks and does the most important ones first.	Good	Middle 20%
2 points	Does the most important tasks first.		Poor	Next 20%
1 point	Does tasks as they come. Asks his or her superior.	Uses no system.	Unacceptable	Bottom 20%

The descriptors for these four scales were developed to evaluate the question: "Establishing priorities and planning are important aspects of the job. Can you give an example from your experience where you established priorities and planned your work?" Adapted from Campion *et al.* (1997), p. 676.

a) The **first** type is composed of scales in which the descriptors are **examples of behaviours** or responses by the interviewee. Of course, these are but examples in which the terms can differ from those used by the candidate.

b) The descriptors of the **second** type of scale correspond to elements of the definition of the evaluated criterion or its **indicators.** This kind of scale is similar to the first one, except that the descriptors are more **generic.** Types 1 and 2 are called behaviourally anchored rating scales.

c) The **third** type of scale simply uses **adjectives** as descriptors.

d) Finally, the **fourth** type of scale **compares** the person under evaluation to the other candidates.

Recommended scales. **Behaviourally anchored** rating scales that use behavioural examples (Type 1) are well suited to situational, behavioural or knowledge questions, especially when the evaluation is done by questions. Behaviourally anchored rating scales that use the criterion definition or its indicators (Type 2) are applicable to all kinds of questions, as long as the evaluation is done by selection criteria. The **adjective**-type scale (Type 3) can be used with all kinds of questions, ideally after each criterion evaluated has been defined and its indicators determined.

Behaviourally anchored rating scales, more objective than the others, should also be more reliable, which may be very advantageous in the event of a dispute or litigation. Research in general, including that from the performance evaluation field, confirms the value of behaviourally anchored scales, though without demonstrating their systematic superiority in relation to less structured scales such as the adjective type.[13]

Using **comparison**-type scales (Type 4) is to be avoided[14] because the evaluation is always relative to the reference group. The best candidate in a group may not meet the job requirements, especially if the group is particularly low-skilled. In addition, since the candidates must be evaluated as soon as possible after each interview (notes are never completely exhaustive, and it is better to begin the evaluation before any relevant information is forgotten), a person cannot be compared to candidates who have not yet been interviewed.

In short, behaviourally anchored rating scales are recommended, as well as simpler scales that use descriptive adjectives.

---

13. See Campion *et al.* (1997).
14. Taylor and O'Driscoll (1995).

Number of gradations. Most grading scales used in research and in practice have four to seven gradations. The maximum number is nine.[15] It is futile to use a scale with gradations that are finer than the precision that can be achieved with an interview – its precision would only be an illusion.

An example of a scale with adjectival anchors. Figure 5.1 illustrates an example of a grading scale with adjectival descriptors.

FIGURE 5.1

Example of a scale with adjectival anchors

Unacceptable Does not meet job requirements	Poor Barely meets job requirements	Good Fully satisfies job requirements for adequate performance	Very good Slightly exceeds job requirements	Excellent Clearly exceeds job requirements
1	2	3	4	5

This kind of scale requires a large measure of judgment from its users. On the other hand, only having to use four or five levels allows the evaluators to set the scales more easily, especially after interviewing a certain number of candidates. It should also be remembered that if you are dealing with an evaluation by criteria, these have been defined and their indicators determined in advance, which helps to structure the evaluation and increase objectivity.

SUPPLEMENTARY NOTATIONS

Notations can be made during the evaluation of a criterion or a question in order to make the meaning more precise, although they are not obligatory. The following are examples of supplementary notations.[16]

15. See Dipboye (1992).
16. Taken in part from Byham (1987).

(+) or (–): *Slightly above* (+) *or below* (–) *the score.* Sometimes a candidate falls between two scores on the scale used. This can be indicated with a + or a – beside the score (e.g., 3+, 5–) or by using half points (e.g., 3.5, 4.5).

(*I*): *Information incomplete or ambiguous.* An (I) can indicate that the interviewer is not sure about the score assigned, either because too little information was received, or because the information was ambiguous (e.g., 3I, 2I).

(*5/2*): *Split score.* A split score is given to a candidate who has different, even contradictory, behaviours in separate but comparable situations. For example, the person might give responses that show a high sensitivity to clients' needs and expectations. On the other hand, the person may seem a great deal less open about the needs of his or her own employees. The candidate therefore could receive a score of 5/2 for the Sensitivity criterion - 5 in relation to clients and 2 for subordinates. A split score indicates that a selection criterion was not properly defined, that it combines two independent dimensions and is therefore not homogeneous. (See *Step 2, Determining and defining the selection criteria.*)

FACTORS THAT CAN DISTORT THE EVALUATION

In spite of all the precautions taken to ensure that the interview is as objective as possible (e.g., systematic job analysis, defining selection criteria and determining indicators, standardizing the questions and the conduct of the interview, taking notes, standardizing the evaluation process), factors remain that can influence the interviewers' judgment without their realizing it, and thus distort the evaluations and the resulting decisions. Understanding these factors is a first step towards objectivity.

1. *The candidate's attributes.* It has frequently been demonstrated that the **physical appearance of the candidate** (e.g., height, weight, dress, hair style) influences the interviewers' judgment.[17]

17. See Eder and Harris (1999); Gatewood and Feild (2001); Posthuma *et al.* (2002); Hosoda *et al.* (2003).

For example, overweight people tend to be evaluated less favourably, while clean clothes and a professional appearance are generally associated with more positive evaluations. Some **demographic characteristics**, such as age, sex and race, also affect the evaluation.[18]

When these personal or demographic characteristics have nothing to do with the criteria being evaluated and are a reflection of bias, they are called *stereotypes.*[19] For example, the belief that men are too proud to take a particular job is an unfounded bias.

There is another kind of error, called the *similar-to-me* error, according to which candidates tend to be evaluated more favourably when they have the same demographic characteristics as the interviewer, or if they share the interviewer's opinions or attitudes.[20]

2. *Candidate's non-verbal behaviour.* The candidate's non-verbal signs during the interview (e.g., eye contact, smiles and other facial expressions, nodding of the head, gestures, posture, tone of voice, spatial distance) have the power to influence the interviewer.[21] Taking the candidate's non-verbal behaviours into consideration during evaluation is not prohibited. However, two conditions must be met: *a*) these behaviours must be treated in the same way as the other indicators and included in the evaluation sheet, and *b*) their validity must be reasonably demonstrated.[22] You must be particularly vigilant with regard to cultural differences. For example, avoiding eye contact or not shaking the committee members' hands can wrongly be associated with a lack of interpersonal skills, when in fact it might only be normal practice for a person from another culture.

18. See Eder and Harris (1999); Gatewood and Feild (2001); Posthuma *et al.* (2002).
19. Canada Revenue Agency (1992).
20. See Gatewood and Feild (2001); Posthuma *et al.* (2002).
21. See Eder and Harris (1999); Gatewood and Feild (2001); Posthuma *et al.* (2002).
22. Using a validation approach based on content or on an external criterion.

3. *Inappropriate weighting of information.* **Negative** information tends to have a greater influence on evaluations than positive information, especially for criteria related to morality.[23] This is frequently observed and may be explained by the interviewer's natural tendency towards self-protection: to recommend a candidate who is not appropriate for the job is usually a more visible mistake (and more damaging to the interviewer's reputation) than not recommending a competent person.

   In the same way, information received at the **beginning of the interview** often has more weight than subsequent information,[24] which gives rise to the well-known *first impressions* phenomenon, according to which some interviewers have a natural tendency to make a judgment about the candidate in the first few minutes. These interviewers form an opinion very early on, and then try to confirm it afterwards. Information received before the interview can have the same effect (e.g., comments from a former boss, results on an examination).

4. *Halo effect.* Another mistake is the halo effect. This occurs when the candidate's good or bad evaluation on one criterion influences and unduly determines the evaluation of other criteria.[25] For example, an interviewer who has favourably evaluated a person on verbal communication may automatically think that the person is competent and motivated.

5. *Contrast effect.* The contrast effect may happen when a candidate is evaluated in comparison to previously interviewed candidates, rather than against a predetermined scale like a grading scale anchored on behaviours or adjectives. A person interviewed immediately after a candidate whose interview was seen as poor may, in comparison, receive a higher score than would have been given if the previous candidate had impressed the interviewers.[26]

23. See Gatewood and Feild (2001); Posthuma *et al.* (2002).
24. See Gatewood and Feild (2001); Taylor and O'Driscoll (1995).
25. See Gatewood and Feild (2001); Taylor and O'Driscoll (1995).
26. Canada Revenue Agency (1992); Taylor and O'Driscoll (1995).

6. *Effect of time and practice.* The simple passage of time may affect the evaluations. For example, it may be that the interviewers are less severe (or more severe) in their evaluations at the end of the day than at the beginning, because they are tired or because they are adhering less strictly to the scale.

   As the interviews continue, the interviewers become more familiar with the evaluation tools (i.e., the selection criteria definitions, the indicators and the grading scales) and they may apply them differently than they did to the first people interviewed.[27]

7. *The requirements of different interviewers.* Interviewers do not all have the same requirements when they evaluate a person. Some are very tough and always on the lookout for any negative piece of information. These people often tend to give low scores. Others are very indulgent and their scores are higher.[28] These deviations may depend on the interviewer's expectations and his or her conception of the ideal candidate.[29]

Solutions. It is not easy to avoid these errors and counteract these natural tendencies. Nevertheless, some steps can be taken to guard against them. For example, the interviewer should:

- Follow the prepared interview guide methodically.
- Pay close attention to the candidate's answers and make note of facts and observations.
- Evaluate each person immediately after the interview, using the rating scale and leaving aside, for the moment, consideration of the other people who have already been evaluated.
- Review the scores assigned periodically (e.g., at the end of each day, or after every five interviews) to ensure the evaluation tools are being used uniformly.
- Use a selection committee made up of several evaluators who are the same for all candidates.

27. Canada Revenue Agency (1992).
28. Olson (1980); Taylor and O'Driscoll (1995).
29. See Posthuma *et al.* (2002).

EVALUATION BY COMMITTEE

A committee with several evaluators makes it possible to neutralize errors arising from personal biases like *stereotyping*, the *similar-to-me* error and personal requirements.[30] With a selection committee, it is recommended that the scores from each member of the committee be collated in a **three-phase process** (see below).[31] This process can occur at the end of each interview, after a certain number of interviews (e.g., at the end of a day of interviewing) or only after all the interviews have been conducted. However, waiting until the end of all the interviews before evaluating may cause serious problems when there are many interviews or they take place over a long time period. If such is the case, all the notes must be reread in order to remember each candidate, which takes longer.[32]

Phase 1: Individual preparation. Each evaluator or interviewer should individually complete their **interview notes** for each interviewee. These notes include responses, facts and observations normally relating to selection criteria, their indicators, and expected responses. The evaluator records this information in the interview guide or the evaluation sheet, and organizes it by questions or criteria, according to the approach selected. Finally, the interviewer proceeds individually to the **evaluation** for each question or selection criterion, whichever approach is being used.

Phase 2: Sharing information. All the interviewers then pool the results for each candidate as follows: beginning with the first criterion (or question) evaluated, each interviewer in turn gives an evaluation and then justifies it with the information noted. For example, Interviewer 1 could talk about the favourable information (facts and observations) justifying his score of 4, but also the unfavourable elements that prevented him from giving a higher score of 5. It is not necessary to

30. Using several evaluators has several other advantages; these are outlined in *Step 4, Conducting an Interview by Committee.*
31. See Byham (1987); Taylor and O'Driscoll (1995)
32. According to Campion, Palmer and Campion (1997, section 13), current research does not allow us to determine the best time to do the evaluation. They suggest, however, that this aspect should not be critical if the interview process is structured and the interviewers well trained.

talk about all the elements when, for instance, they have already been mentioned by another interviewer. The other interviewers listen, add to their notes as needed and may even reconsider their evaluation in light of the discussion.

Phase 3: The committee's evaluation. When all the evaluators have presented their justifications for one selection criterion or question, they decide, as a group this time, on the final score to be given, based on all the information available.

Reaching a consensus. Ideally, the evaluators should assign a final score by consensus for each selection criterion or question. It is believed that consensus makes for a fairer evaluation than a simple addition of the interviewers' scores (or their average), because during the discussion, the evaluation with the best support should win everyone over. Even though research results seem to indicate that the results of evaluations by consensus are only slightly superior, this is not really the case for structured interviews.[33] Consequently, it is better to try and reach a consensus. But if this proves to be difficult, the average for all the evaluations for each criterion or question can be assigned.

OVERALL EVALUATION SHEET

It is useful to fill out an overall evaluation sheet for each candidate and to record the following information:

- evaluation of each criterion or question according to the method chosen;
- overall evaluation, where applicable (see *Step 6*);
- justification of the evaluations with the facts and observations recorded.

33. See Campion *et al.* (1997); Pulakos *et al.* (1996).

STEP 6

MAKING THE DECISION

Making the decision is the last step of the process. At a certain point, the time comes to decide which of the people evaluated is the most suitable for the position, or which of these people are most suitable to continue in the selection process (see Table 0.3, *The steps in the selection interview*).

The interview is frequently used in combination with other selection tools (e.g., a knowledge test or psychometric tests). You must remember that this book only deals with the interview, and its goal is not to describe all the many methods (overall score, multiple cut-off score, multiple hurdle processes with or without an accumulation of scores), or consider their complex ramifications, for integrating the results of several selection tools in order to make a decision.

Therefore we will outline a few suggestions about the way to use the evaluations obtained from interviews, because these must be integrated in order to make it possible to decide whether the candidates will move on to the next step in the selection process. Without going into detail, two major approaches are available to an organization: putting together an overall score for each candidate or setting a cut-off score for each criterion or question evaluated.

OVERALL SCORE

Calculating a candidate's overall score can be done mathematically or clinically.

Mathematical method. With the mathematical method, the evaluations by question or selection criteria are combined to establish an overall score by **mechanically** following a pre-established formula that is in most cases the sum or the average of the evaluations. Using this method, it is possible to give more weight to some questions or criteria, depending on the job requirements. If the overall score is based on the sum of the questions, you can use the number of questions per criterion to reflect the desired weighting.

Clinical method. With the clinical method, combining the evaluations is based on the **judgment** of the interviewers. First they look at the evaluations obtained and their relative importance to the job, then they give the candidate an overall score. It should be noted that a simple overall score, without a previous evaluation of questions or criteria, i.e., with very little structure, is not advised. (See *Step 5, Standardizing the Evaluation.*)

Recommended method. Many studies, although not all, prefer the mathematical method because of its objectivity and its presumed effect on the reliability and validity of results.[1] Contrary to expectations, however, **weighting** the evaluations obtained for the selection criteria (or questions) does not necessarily increase the validity of the

1. See Campion *et al.* (1997); Gatewood and Feild (2001); Taylor and O'Driscoll (1995).

results.[2] Consequently, weighting is not recommended, unless there is a clear indication for it, based on the job analysis, such as one criterion being twice as important as another.[3] Weighting the criteria must be based on the importance of the tasks and other aspects of the job to be filled, particularly in relation to their frequency and their consequences.[4]

Underlying justification of the method. Calculating an overall score is based implicitly on the logic that a candidate can compensate for a weakness in one selection criterion with strength in another. In the example shown in Table 6.1, Josie shows a serious weakness in the Leadership criterion, but she has the best overall score because the two other criteria have compensated for her weakness in Leadership.

TABLE 6.1

Evaluation of three candidates (on a scale of 1 to 5)

	Dimensions evaluated			
Persons evaluated	Leadership	Teamwork	Oral expression	Overall score
Mario	3	3	3	3.00
Caroline	4	3	3	3.33
Josie	1	5	5	3.67

In certain cases, it is indeed possible for the strength of one criterion to compensate for a weakness in another. For example, an aptitude for learning and a great deal of motivation may counterbalance more limited job knowledge, but this is not always the case. A facility for oral expression cannot make up for a lack of leadership, for instance. Situations may arise when a weakness on one criterion is aggravated by the strength of another. For example, if a candidate shows inadequate judgment, the consequences of his or her actions may be more harmful if there is also a tendency to take initiative.

2. See Campion *et al.* (1997); Dipboye (1992).
3. Taylor and O'Driscoll (1995).
4. Pettersen (2000).

A CUT-OFF SCORE FOR EACH SELECTION CRITERION

Instead of calculating an overall score, the other approach is to set a cut-off score for each criterion or question evaluated in the interview. To be hired, or allowed to continue the selection process, a candidate must obtain evaluations equal to or greater than each threshold. The cut-off score may vary from one criterion to another, because they reflect the job requirements.[5] It is also possible to set cut-off score for a group of criteria or questions: one passing score for all the criteria related to interpersonal qualities, for example, another for the criteria related to knowledge, etc.

Underlying justification of the method. In the preceding example (see Table 6.1), if a cut-off score of 3 had been set for each criterion, Josie would have been rejected and the other two candidates would have qualified. Josie's strength in the other selection criteria would not have compensated for her weakness in Leadership this time. If we follow the logic of this multiple cut-off scores, each criterion or group of criteria is deemed essential for the job, no matter what evaluations are obtained for the other criteria.

MIXED SYSTEMS

Various combinations of the two preceding methods can be envisaged. The following are a few examples.

a) Set cut-off scores for all the selection criteria measured in the interview and then calculate an overall score for those people who reach those cut-offs.

b) Set cut-off scores only for certain selection criteria that are deemed essential for the job, then calculate an overall score combining all the selection criteria only for those candidates who have attained those cut-offs.

5. To learn more about how to determine thresholds, see Cascio *et al.* (1989); Cronbach (1990); Gatewood and Feild (2001).

c) Having calculated an overall score, set a cut-off for this overall score.

d) Calculate the overall score and set a cut-off for this overall score, then select the people who have obtained the highest overall scores in top-down order until you have reached a pre-set number (e.g., the number of positions available), as long as they have attained the cut-off.

In the end, do not forget that the overall score is in turn combined with the scores obtained in the other selection tools.

OTHER CONSIDERATIONS

In terms of the process, it is not always easy to make a decision whether to recommend a candidate or not. Following are two examples of a delicate situation. The suggested solutions are only possible in situations where the likelihood of legal dispute is practically nil. Otherwise, you must keep to the decision rules set at the beginning of the process. (See *Step 2*.)

Example 1: Two satisfactory candidates, one job. The evaluations are finished and the committee members are having difficulty choosing between two candidates. There is only one position to be filled. In spite of long discussions, they have not been able to reach a decision. What is to be done? If, in fact, the two candidates have practically the **same profile** of competencies according to the evaluations, other selection criteria, like complementary job competences or proximity of residence, that are not essential but relevant to the job could be added to differentiate between them.[6] If they still seem equal, another step could be added, like a further interview or an oral presentation.

On the other hand, what do you do if the candidates have **different competency profiles** so that each of them has strong and weak points distinguishing them? For instance, suppose Candidate A has great lead-

6. It is essential, however, to avoid any grounds for unlawful discrimination.

ership qualities but not enough knowledge in the field of expertise required for the job, while Candidate B, whose leadership level is merely adequate, has a great deal of knowledge in that field. However, the selection of either candidate will have repercussions in the organization. For example, if the current employees do not have a great deal of expertise, it would be preferable to choose Candidate B, to avoid the risk of a serious reduction in the quality of products and services. However, if the current employees have a great deal of expertise in the field but do not work together well, Candidate A might be the one chosen. In fact, the solution to this dilemma usually requires that you go back to the job analysis, its context, requirements and *raison d'être*, and if that is not enough, to the organization's strategic plan.

Example 2: No candidate is satisfactory. The committee realizes that none of the candidates evaluated fully satisfies the job requirements. To resolve this difficulty, the following question must be answered: are there qualified candidates that did not apply and is it possible to recruit them? If it is **possible**, then the selection process must begin all over again, in particular the recruitment phase, even if that is often hard to live with because of the following unfortunate consequences: *a*) a longer delay before the position is filled, *b*) the need for additional financial and human resources, *c*) the perception that those responsible for the selection process failed in their job, and *d*) the awful job of telling the candidates that they did not meet the requirements for the position, which is especially difficult with internal candidates. Starting the process again, therefore, requires a certain amount of courage.

On the other hand, if it is believed to be **impossible** to attract better candidates, two alternatives remain: *a*) leave the position vacant temporarily, or *b*) hire the most qualified candidate in the current circumstances. Make sure that you rationally weigh the disadvantages of each of these possibilities. If you opt for the second alternative, and decide to hire a candidate that does not meet all the job requirements, some compensatory measures must be considered. For example, you could provide for training or support for the chosen candidate, or modify the job and its responsibilities in relation to that person's competencies, knowing that the incumbent may never achieve the desired performance levels. You must realistically consider the probability of the candidate's improvement, given that certain behaviours or character traits are more difficult than others to acquire. For example, decisiveness, dynamism or the tendency to overlook consideration for others are character traits that will not change after some development sessions from management or a few hours of training. Sometimes we tend to overestimate the ability of the adult to adapt.

CONCLUSION

The structured interview is not the only effective way of conducting a selection interview. Qualified interviewers, such as psychologists and other experienced personnel selection specialists, achieve remarkable results using more flexible types of interviews, relying more on judgment, expertise and even, at times, on intuition.[1] However, for the majority of interviewers and in most circumstances, the structured, job-related interview remains the most dependable kind of interview for evaluating job candidates. By virtue of its higher reliability and validity indices, it represents a profitable investment for organizations and a fair means of evaluation for candidates. Too many organizations

1. For example, see the recommendations in the field of selection made by Jack Welch (2005), based on 21 years in control at General Electric.

have not yet made use of this technique, but its many advantages should give decision makers food for thought, since they make up for its disadvantages and refute the most common objections to its use.

Obviously it is up to each organization to determine the preferred form of the interview in relation to its particular situation, and the highest levels of structure need not always be selected. For example, an organization that often has to face legal challenges might lean towards the maximum level of structure, but another company not subject to the same kind of pressures would be justified in opting for a lower level of structure.

The selection interview is a constantly evolving field of practice and research. Over fifty years of research has contributed to the establishment of rules and practices that have greatly improved the effectiveness of this selection tool. But it would be an illusion to consider these ways of doing things as immutable. We must always be looking for improvement. New interview practices, new knowledge, changes to the legal framework and the evolution of case law, constant progress in information technology, to name just a few examples, must continually be factored into the equation.

FURTHER READING

Berman, J.A. (1997). *Competence-based Employment Interviewing*. Westport: Quorum Books.

Campion, M.A., Palmer, D.K., & Campion, J.E. (1997). A review of structure in the selection interview. *Personnel Psychology, 50*, 655–702.

Dipboye, R.L. (1992). *Selection interviews: Process Perspectives*. Cincinnati: South-Western Publishing.

Eder, R.W., & Harris, M.M. (dir.). (1999). *The Employment Interview Handbook*. Newbury Park: Sage.

Gatewood, R.D., & Feild, H.S. (2001). *Human Resource Selection* (5th ed.). Fort Worth: Harcourt.

Posthuma, R.A., Morgeson, F.P., & Campion, M.A. (2002). Beyond employment interview validity: A comprehensive narrative review of recent research and trends over time. *Personnel Psychology, 55*, 1–81.

Taylor, P.J., & O'Driscoll, M.P. (1995). *Structured Employment Interviewing*. Aldershot: Gower.

REFERENCES

American Educational Research Association, American Psychological Association, & National Council on Measurement in Education (1999). *Standards for Educational and Psychological Testing*. Washington: American Psychological Association.

Berge, Z., DeVerneil, M., Berge, N., Davis, L., & Smith, D. (2002). The increasing scope of training and development competency. *Benchmarking: An International Journal*, *9*(1), 43–61.

Brannick, M.T., & Levine, E.L. (2002). *Job Analysis*. Thousand Oaks: Sage.

Breaugh, J.A. (2000). Research on employee recruitment: So many studies, so many remaining questions. *Journal of Management*, *26*(3), 405–30.

Burnett, J.R., Fan, C., Motowildo, S.J., & Degroot, T. (1998). Interview notes and validity. *Personnel Psychology, 51*, 375–96.

Byham, W.C. (1987). *Sélection ciblée* (rev. ed.). Pittsburgh: Development Dimensions International.

Campion, M.A., Palmer, D.K., & Campion, J.E. (1997). A review of structure in the selection interview. *Personnel Psychology, 50*, 655–702.

Canada Revenue Agency (1992). *Atelier sur l'entrevue axée sur le comportement – Manuel du participant.* Ottawa: Politique et planification, Direction générale des ressources humaines.

Cascio, W.F., Alexander, R.A., & Barrett, G.V. (1989). Setting cutoff scores: Legal, psychometric, and professional issues and guideline. *Personnel Psychology, 41*, 1–24.

Catano, V.M., Cronshaw, S.F., Wiesner, W.H., Hackett, R.D., & Méthot, L.L. (1997). *Recruitment and Selection in Canada.* Scarborough: ITP Nelson.

Commission de la fonction publique du Québec. *Guide d'application des décisions de la Commission de la fonction publique.*

Commission de la fonction publique du Québec. (2002). *Rapport annuel d'activités 2001-2002.* Québec: Les Publications du Québec.

Conway, J.M., Jako, R.A., & Goodman, D.F. (1995). A meta-analysis of interrater and internal consistency reliability of selection interviews. *Journal of Applied Psychology, 80*, 565–79.

Cook, M. (1993). *Personnel Selection and Productivity.* Chichester: Wiley.

Cronbach, L.J. (1990). *Essentials of Psychological Testing* (5th ed.). New York: HarperCollins, 418–20.

Dingle, J. (1995). Analyzing the competence requirements of managers. *Management Development Review, 8*(2), 30–7.

Dipboye, R.L. (1992). *Selection interviews: Process Perspectives.* Cincinnati: South-Western Publishing.

Dubnicki, C., & Williams, J.B. (1990). Selecting and developing outstanding performers. *Healthcare Forum Journal,* Nov.-Dec., 28–34.

Durivage, A. (2004). La gestion des compétences et le processus de sélection du Mouvement Desjardins. *Gestion, 29*(1), 10–18.

Durivage, A., & Thibault, J. (2000). La mesure des compétences à l'aide de l'entrevue «Architecte de recrutement» - Descriptif, mesure et développement. In B. Gangloff (ed.), *Les compétences professionnelles*. Paris: L'Harmattan.

Eder, R.W., & Harris, M.M. (ed.). (1999). *The Employment Interview handbook*. Newbury Park: Sage.

Farnham, D., & Stevens, A. (2000). Developing and implementing competence-based recruitment and selection in a social services department - A case study of West Sussex County Council. *The International Journal of Public Sector Management*, *13*(4), 369–82.

Flanagan, J.C. (1954). The critical incident technique. *Psychological Bulletin*, *51*, 327–55.

Gatewood, R.D., & Feild, H.S. (2001). *Human Resource Selection* (5th ed.). Fort Worth: Harcourt.

Goldstein, I.L., Zedeck, S., & Schneider, B. (1993). An exploration of the job analysis-content validity process. In N. Schmitt, W.C. Borman and Associates (ed.), *Personnel selection in organization*. San Francisco: Jossey-Bass, 3–34.

Guion, R.M. (1998). *Assessment, Measurement, and Prediction for Personnel Decisions*. Mahwah: Lawrence Erlbaum Associates.

Haccoun, R., Rigny, A.J., & Bordeleau, Y. (1979). Une nouvelle approche en recrutement et en gestion: la description réaliste de l'emploi (DRE). *Commerce*, sept., 54–63.

Harris, M.M. (1989). Reconsidering the employment interview: A review of recent literature and suggestions for future research. *Personnel Psychology*, *42*, 691–726.

Hausknecht, J.P., Day, D.V., & Thomas, S.C. (2004). Applicant reactions to selection procedures: An updated model and meta-analysis. *Personnel Psychology*, *57*, 639–83.

Hoffman, T. (1999). The meaning of competency. *Journal of European Industrial Training*, *23*(6), 275–85.

Hosoda, M., Stone-Romero, E.F., & Coats, G. (2003). The effects of physical attractiveness on job-related outcomes: A meta-analysis of experimental studies. *Personnel Psychology*, *56*, 431–62.

Huffcutt, A.I., & Arthur Jr, W. (1994). Hunter and Hunter (1984) revisited: Interview validity for entry-level jobs. *Journal of Applied Psychology, 79*, 184–90.

Huffcutt, A.I., Roth, P.L., & McDaniel, M.A. (1996). A meta-analytic investigation of cognitive ability in employment interview evaluation: Moderating characteristics and implications for incremental validity. *Journal of Applied Psychology, 81*, 459–73.

Huffcutt, A.I., & Woehr, D.J. (1999). Further analysis of employment interview validity: A quantitative evaluation of interviewer-related structuring methods. *Journal of Organizational Behavior, 20*, 549–60.

Hunter, J.E. (1986). Cognitive ability, cognitive aptitudes, job knowledge, and job performance. *Journal of Vocational Behavior, 29*(3), 340–62.

Hunter, J.E., & Hunter, R.F. (1984). Validity and utility of alternative predictors of job performance. *Psychological Bulletin, 96*(1), 72–98.

Janz, T., Hellervick, L., & Gilmore, D.C. (1986). *Behavior Description Interviewing*. Boston: Allyn and Bacon.

Lasnier, F. (2000). *Réussir la formation par compétences*. Montréal: Guérin.

Lawler III, E.E., Ledford Jr., G.E., & Chang, L. (1993) Who uses skill-based pay and why. *Compensation and Benefits Review, 2*(5), 22–6.

Lombardo, M.M., & Eichinger, R.W. (1995). *Manuel de l'architecte de recrutement*. Minneapolis: Lominger.

Marchese, M.C., & Muchinsky, P.M. (1993). The validity of the employment interview: A meta-analysis. *International Journal of Selection and Assessment, 1*(1), 18–26.

May, A. (1999). Developing management competencies for fast-changing organizations. *Career Development International, 4*(6), 336–9.

McDaniel, M.A., Whetzel, D.L., Schmidt, F.L., & Maurer, S.D. (1994). The validity of employment interview: A comprehensive review and meta-analysis. *Journal of Applied Psychology, 79*, 599–616.

Milkovich, G.T., & Newman, J.M. (1999). *Compensation*. Boston: McGraw-Hill.

Olson, R.F. (1980). *Managing the Interview: A Self-teaching Guide*. New York: Wiley.

Pettersen, N. (2000). *Évaluation du potentiel humain dans les organisations*. Québec: Presses de l'Université du Québec.

Pettersen, N., & Jacob, R. (1992). *Comprendre le comportement de l'individu au travail: un schéma d'organisation*. Laval: Éditions Agence d'Arc.

Posthuma, R.A., Morgeson, F.P., & Campion, M.A. (2002). Beyond employment interview validity: A comprehensive narrative review of recent research and trends over time. *Personnel Psychology, 55*, 1–81.

Public Service Commission of Canada (2004). *Standards for Selection and Assessment*. Ottawa: Public Service Commission, Government of Canada. <www.psc.gc.ca>, accessed September 27, 2004.

Pulakos, E.D., Schmitt, N., Whitney, D., & Smith, M. (1996). Individual differences in interviewer ratings: The impact of standardization, consensus discussion, and sampling error on the validity of structured interview. *Personnel Psychology, 49*, 85–102.

Rowe, C. (1995). Clarifying the use of competence and competency models in recruitment, assessment and staff development. *Industrial and Commercial Training, 27*(11), 12–17.

Schmidt, F.L., & Hunter, J.E. (1998). The validity of selection methods in personnel psychology: Practical and theoritical implications of 85 years of research findings. *Psychological Bulletin, 124*, 262–74.

Schmitt, N., & Chan, D. (1998). *Personnel Selection*. Thousand Oaks: Sage.

Secrétariat du Conseil du trésor (2001). *Module 2 – L'analyse d'emploi à des fins de sélection*. Québec: Gouvernement du Québec.

Shippmann, J.S., Ash, R.A., Battista, M., Carr, L., Eyde, L.D., Pearlman, K., & Prien, E.P. (2000). The practice of competency modeling. *Personnel Psychology, 53*, 703–40.

Slinvinski, L.W., & Miles, J. (1997). *Wholistic Competency Model: A Profile*. Ottawa: Public Service Commission of Canada.

Society for Industrial and Organizational Psychology (2003). *Principles for Validation and Use of Personnel Selection Procedures* (4th ed.). College Park: American Psychological Association.

Spencer, L.M., & Spencer, S.M. (1993). *Competence at Work*. New York: Wiley.

Taylor, P.J., & O'Driscoll, M.P. (1995). *Structured Employment Interviewing*. Aldershot, Hampshire: Gower.

Terpstra, D.E., Mohamed, A.A., & Kethley, R.B. (1999). An analysis of federal court cases involving nine selection devices. *International Journal of Selection and Assessment*, *7*(1), 26–34.

Tett, R.P., Guterman, H.A., Bleier, A., & Murphy, P.J. (2000). Development and content validation of a "hyperdimensional" taxonomy of managerial competence. *Human Performance*, *13*(3), 205–51.

Tovey, L. (1994). Competency assessment – A strategic approach Part II. *Executive Development*, *7*(1), 16–19.

Van Der Zee, K.I., Baker, A.B., & Baker, P. (2002). Why are structured interviews so rarely used in personnel selection? *Journal of Applied Psychology*, *87*(1), 176–87.

Welch, J. (2005). *Winning*. New York: HarperCollins.

Weisner, W.H., & Cronshaw, S.F. (1988). A meta-analytic investigation of the impact of interview format and degree of structure on the validity of the employment interview. *Journal of Occupational Psychology*, *61*, 275–90.

Wilk, S.L., & Cappelli, P. (2003). Understanding the determinants of employer use of selection methods. *Personnel Psychology*, *56*, 103–24.

Wright, P.M., Lichtenfels, P.A., & Pursell, E.D. (1989). The structured interview: Additional studies and meta-analysis. *Journal of Occupational Psychology*, *62*, 191–9.

APPENDIX

A

EXAMPLE OF A JOB DESCRIPTION FOR SELECTION PURPOSES

Job Title: Store Manager			
JOB IDENTIFICATION			
Classification	Director, level 1	**Line supervisor**	Regional Director
Administrative unit	Store	**Job code**	1262-11

JOB SUMMARY	HIERARCHICAL POSITION
➢ Provides customer service ➢ Stimulates sales ➢ Manages operating costs ➢ Supervises sales personnel ➢ Gets involved in the community ➢ Supports the District Director in business development	**Executives (Board of Directors)** ↓ **Vice-Presidents (States-Provinces)** ↓ **General Directors (Products)** ↓ **Regional Directors (Regions)** ↓ **Store Manager (Store)**

WHAT NEEDS TO BE DONE	
Responsibility 1: Personalized service	**Responsibility 2: Staff performance**
TASKS *a*) Listens to customers' expectations and makes sure that employees and him- or herself respond to them appropriately. *b*) Upholds the company's standards for presentation, cleanliness and customer services. *c*) Ensures that products are available to customers. *d*) Keeps up to date on market trends, sales techniques and the organization's promotional campaigns.	**TASKS** *a*) Establishes a work atmosphere that fosters employee performance. *b*) Establishes and evaluates individual and group performance objectives. *c*) Involves employees and encourages commitment and accountability. *d*) Makes sure to have the required number of competent staff in relation to sales volume fluctuations. *e*) Encourages employee development and ensures that employees maintain appropriate skill levels. *f*) Maintains a safe work environment.
Responsibility 3: Profitability	**Responsibility 4: Community involvement**
TASKS *a*) Ensures market development, implements promotion programs and manages sales. *b*) Works with the District Director to achieve optimal profitability. *c*) Manages the store's financial, material and technological resources. *d*) Manages inventories and ensures optimal stock rotation. *e*) Establishes and manages employee wages.	**TASKS** *a*) Takes part in local business associations. *b*) Establishes business partnerships suited to the division's needs. *c*) Participates in local community activities that contribute to the successful operation of the store. *d*) Encourages local community activities with an advertising budget for that purpose.

EXPECTED OUTCOMES	
Results: Personalised service	**Results: Staff performance**
a) Satisfaction levels of 90% or higher in annual customer satisfaction surveys. *b)* "Normal" or "superior" ratings maintained in biannual inspections.	*a)* Satisfaction levels of 80% or higher in annual employee surveys. *b)* Turnover rate below 20% a year. *c)* Level of unjustified absenteeism less than three days a year per employee.
Results: Profitability	**Results: Community involvement**
a) Yearly gross profit margin before tax of 10% or higher.	*a)* Active participation in three local community associations. *b)* Participation in three community activities a year.

JOB CONTEXT	
Physical environment	
a) Restricted space, facilities being designed to maximize product display. *b)* Each store has an enclosed, windowless office (8' by 8') for administrative work. *c)* Artificial lighting (neon) is standard and the salespeople must share the sales counter. *d)* A small warehouse makes it possible to store the most popular merchandise. *e)* The building is kept at a constant, comfortable temperature to keep merchandise in good condition. *f)* The buildings are clean. *g)* Background music from a local radio station plays quietly during opening hours.	
Working conditions	
Work schedule	Monday: 8:30 am to 5:30 pm Tuesday: 8:30 am to 5:30 pm Wednesday: 8:30 am to 5:30 pm Thursday: 8:30 am to 9:00 pm Friday: 8:30 am to 9:00 pm Saturday: 8:30 am to 5:00 pm
Vacations	One day a week (Monday, Tuesday or Wednesday). Three weeks paid vacation a year. Statutory holidays established by law.
Compensation	Salary of $15.00 to $17.00 an hour according to seniority. 2% salary increase a year thereafter. Annual bonus, determined by the company on the basis of performance (varies between $0 and $5000).
Work contracts	Indeterminate Six-month probation period

Administrative environment	
a) The incumbent must fill out many administrative forms (sales and purchase reports, inventory control, attendance records). *b*) Forms must be turned in each week to ensure the proper operation of the payroll and cash-management systems *c*) Weekly contact must be maintained with the Regional Director, more frequently during promotional campaigns. *d*) There is little contact with peers at other stores (semi-annual meetings). *e*) No administrative support is provided. Some courses in accounting and software use are available on request. *f*) Clientele varies according to the period: – In normal periods, the salesperson/customer ratio is 1 to 1. – In peak periods, the salesperson/customer ratio is 1 to 3. – In slow periods, the salesperson/customer ratio is 2 to 1. – Winter is the busiest time, followed by fall, spring and summer.	
Psychological environment	
Stress level *a*) Managers must respond to constant demands from head office, customers and employees. *b*) Managers bear the full responsibility for the proper functioning and profitability of their store. *c*) The stress level varies according to the traffic in the store. **Culture and atmosphere** *a*) The culture is entrepreneurial. Managers are encouraged to improve the financial performance of their store. *b*) Employees feel they are part of the company. A family culture is encouraged. *c*) Interpersonal conflicts are frequently seen between employees, usually relating to work schedules, division of labour, keeping the building clean and orderly, and work status (full- or part-time). **Communications** *a*) The store manager communicates daily with customers and employees. *b*) The incumbent is regularly in contact with the District Director and local providers, and interacts sporadically with community representatives. *c*) The incumbent participates annually in the company's training programs.	
Equipment and technology	
a) Personal computer (accounting software, Word, Excel, Internet and intranet) *b*) Cash register	

APPENDIX B

TOOLS FOR COLLECTING CRITICAL INCIDENTS

EXAMPLE OF A QUESTIONNAIRE FOR COLLECTING CRITICAL INCIDENTS[1]

Questionnaire – Gathering critical incidents

This questionnaire is designed to provide examples of particularly effective or particularly ineffective performance for the position of *Store Manager.* These examples will then be used to prepare employment interview questions.

We are asking you to think of three examples that illustrate how a *Store Manager* acted in a particularly effective way and another three examples of a particularly ineffective behaviour (or poor performance).

These examples must have actually taken place and you should understand them well. Please preserve the anonymity of the people involved by referring to them only by their title or job, not by name.

For each example, describe:

a) the situation faced by the *Store Manager*;

b) what the *Store Manager* actually did; and

c) the consequences or results of his or her actions.

To help you, here is an example from a technician's job.

Situation: *A technician was approached by a colleague who asked him to help him retrieve a lost file, a task that was not part of the technician's regular duties.*

Behaviour: *The technician replied, "You should have kept a backup copy. It's not my responsibility to find other people's lost files."*

Result: *The colleague could not finish his report on time and he never again asked this technician for help.*

1. This questionnaire, adapted from Taylor and O'Driscoll (1995), is designed to gather critical incidents related to the job as a whole. It could be modified to collect incidents regarding one or several particular aspects of the job.

Please describe three examples of effective behaviour and three examples of ineffective behaviour.

<table>
<tr><th colspan="2">First example of effective behaviour</th></tr>
<tr><th>Situation</th><th>Result</th></tr>
<tr><td>A customer asked to see the manager after a purchase he had made from one of the manager's temporary employees. The customer was furious, because the employee had suggested he purchase a product that did not work out for him at all. When he returned to exchange the product, just an hour later, the employee refused to take it back because the seal was broken. The customer pointed out that he had not used the product and reminded the manager that he had been dealing with the store for several years.</td><td rowspan="3">The customer was very satisfied and continued to deal with the company. The employees have greater latitude and little abuse has been noted. The company has acquired a reputation for flexibility that will help increase its customer base.</td></tr>
<tr><th>Behaviour</th></tr>
<tr><td>The manager first explained that the employee had acted in good faith and was following the company's policies. He said, however, that the employee should have shown more flexibility, given the customer's loyalty to the store. He exchanged the product and gave the customer a good discount on a future purchase. He then met with all his employees to discuss the situation. He authorized the employees to make these kinds of exchanges, but indicated that this type of transaction has to be documented and that any abuse on the part of a customer should be reported to him.</td></tr>
</table>

<table>
<tr><th colspan="2">Second example of effective behaviour</th></tr>
<tr><th>Situation</th><th>Result</th></tr>
<tr><td>The Regional Director told the manager that all the stores in the chain had to participate in a promotion campaign to market a new line of natural products. He stressed the importance of this campaign, because the new products were being made by one of the company's subsidiaries.</td><td rowspan="3">The campaign was a complete success and the store had the best sales figures in the district. The exercise was stimulating for the employees, who said they were motivated by the challenge. The employee presentations have continued and now deal with other products sold in the store.</td></tr>
<tr><th>Behaviour</th></tr>
<tr><td>First of all the store manager gathered all the information about the promotion campaign (dates, types of products, characteristics, etc.). Then he organized a meeting for the employees and asked each of them to make suggestions. After the meeting, every employee was responsible for becoming an expert on one of the new products. They each made a presentation to the other employees. Merchandise in the store was moved in order to place the new products in the best locations. Promotional posters were put up and advertising flyers were distributed to customers. Everyone was ready when the new products arrived.</td></tr>
</table>

<table>
<tr><th colspan="2">Third example of effective behaviour</th></tr>
<tr><th>Situation</th><th>Result</th></tr>
<tr><td>A member of a local association contacted the manager about getting a demonstration of natural products. Only one date was possible, and the manager already had a personal activity planned for that date. The local association had only been created a year or so before, and was mostly made up of young people, a clientele that is not strongly inclined to use natural products.</td><td rowspan="3">The manager's presentation was a success. The members of the association volunteer their services to seniors living at home. They gave the seniors the pamphlets, and the seniors began using the natural products. The presentation helped the manager increase his customer base. He also established favourable links with several members of the association.</td></tr>
<tr><th>Behaviour</th></tr>
<tr><td>The manager hesitated at first, but in the end decided to make the presentation at the requested time. He put off his personal appointment. Then he contacted the president of the association to find out about the members' needs. He prepared promotional material and distributed it to the participants.</td></tr>
</table>

<table>
<tr><th colspan="2">First example of ineffective behaviour</th></tr>
<tr><th>Situation</th><th>Result</th></tr>
<tr><td>The company responsible for cleaning the building declared bankruptcy. This company used to wash the floors and windows three times a week, and its bankruptcy happened during one of the store's busiest times.</td><td rowspan="3">This decision created general discontent among the employees, who told the manager they had not been hired to do the cleaning. They did the work grudgingly and the store's cleanliness suffered as a result. Two temporary employees quit because of this decision. The manager had to hire and train new staff, which cost him much more than the amount he saved on cleaning. After this, he subcontracted the cleaning to another specialized firm.</td></tr>
<tr><th>Behaviour</th></tr>
<tr><td>In order to increase profits by reducing maintenance costs, the manager asked employees to take turns cleaning the store's floors and windows. He set up schedules, bought the necessary equipment and showed an example by doing the job himself once every two weeks.</td></tr>
</table>

<table>
<tr><th colspan="2">Second example of ineffective behaviour</th></tr>
<tr><th>Situation</th><th>Result</th></tr>
<tr><td>One of the manager's part-time employees, who was a computer science student at the university, suggested that he purchase some specialized stock-management software.</td><td rowspan="3">Only three weeks after acquiring the software, the temporary employee left the store to take a job with a computer company. The software program was complex and no one knew how to make it work properly. The manager asked the District Director for help, and was informed that software for stock management was going to be installed in his store shortly and that he had to get rid of the software he had bought. The whole thing ended up with a loss of several thousand dollars.</td></tr>
<tr><th>Behaviour</th></tr>
<tr><td>The employee convinced the manager that this software would help him increase the store's efficiency and reduce losses due to outdated products. He bought the software program and asked the employee to train the others and supervise the entry of the necessary data.</td></tr>
</table>

<table>
<tr><th colspan="2">Third example of ineffective behaviour</th></tr>
<tr><th>Situation</th><th>Result</th></tr>
<tr><td>One of the manager's employees asked him for a raise so he could buy a new house. Normally, raises are established annually at a fixed rate of 3.5%. The employee, who was due to receive his annual raise, had been working for the company for two years and wanted a 6% raise.</td><td rowspan="3">The employee told his colleagues about his good luck and they were upset. They then told the manager that this kind of action smacked of patronage and they had a right to equal treatment. They threatened to bring in the union. After long negotiations, he agreed to give all employees a 5% raise, including the employee who made the original request. In spite of this bonus, the work atmosphere was negatively affected for several weeks.</td></tr>
<tr><th>Behaviour</th></tr>
<tr><td>The manager agreed to the requested raise in view of the employee's superior performance. However, he specified that it was an exceptional measure which would not be repeated in subsequent years.</td></tr>
</table>

EXAMPLE OF AN INDIVIDUAL INTERVIEW GUIDE FOR COLLECTING CRITICAL INCIDENTS[2]

1. **Introduction (5 to 10 minutes)**

   [*Establish an atmosphere of trust between interviewer and interviewee.*][3]

   - *Confidentiality of responses*
     It goes without saying that we are committed in all circumstances to ensuring the confidentiality of your responses and preserving the anonymity of anyone you allude to in your responses. Only aggregate results or those not referring to individuals will be revealed.
   - *Permission to record responses*
     With your permission, I would like to record your responses. That will allow me to pay more attention to what you are saying instead of having to take notes continually. However, if you prefer not to be recorded, let me know and I will turn off the machine.

2. Adapted from Spencer and Spencer (1993).
3. Remarks in square brackets are instructions for the interviewer.

2. **Critical incidents (45 minutes)**

This meeting is to identify HOW A *Store Manager* ACTS WHEN DOING THE JOB WELL. The way we do this is to ask you to give examples of what you do at work, and describe some of the most important incidents that have happened to you at work that resulted in the most significant consequences for your company. We are going to ask you to describe three positive incidents and three negative ones in detail.

2.1. Let's begin with three **positive** incidents that had favourable consequences for the company. I would like to have a complete example of the type of things that *you do* in your work. Can you remember a specific moment or situation in your work as a *Store Manager*, an incident where you felt particularly *effective* – an event, a situation, or a critical episode, for example, or a success in your job that was among the most important ones for the company?

Could you please tell us in detail:

a) What the situation was? What led up to it? What were the events and circumstances that preceded this situation?

b) Who was involved?

c) What did you think, feel or want to do in this situation?
[*We want to know:*
- *what the interviewee thought of other people (e.g., whether he or she was positive or negative) or about the situation (e.g., how the problem was solved);*
- *about the interviewee's feelings (e.g., nervous, self-confident); and*
- *what the interviewee wanted to do, his or her motivations (e.g., whether he or she did his best, or wanted to impress others).*]

d) What did you do or say?
[*We want to know what skills and other qualities were demonstrated by the interviewee.*]

e) What happened? What were the results or the consequences of your actions?

2.2. Let's move on to three examples of negative incidents whose consequences were unfavourable for the organization. I would like to have a complete example of the kind of things *you should not have done* in your work. Can you remember a particular moment in you work as *Store Manager*, where you felt particularly *ineffective*? For example, was there an event, a situation, a critical episode, or a failure in your work that was among the most important for the organization?

Can you tell us in detail:

a) What was the situation? What led up to it? What were the events and circumstances that preceded this situation?

b) Who was involved?

c) What did you think, feel or want to do in this situation?
[*We want to know:*
- *what the interviewee thought of other people (e.g., whether he or she was positive or negative) or about the situation (e.g., how the problem was solved);*
- *about the interviewee's feelings (e.g., nervous, self-confident); and*
- *what the interviewee wanted to do, his or her motivations (e.g., whether he or she did his best, or wanted to impress others).*]

d) What did you do or say?
[*We want to know what skills and other qualities were demonstrated by the interviewee.*]

e) What happened? What were the results or the consequences of your actions?

3. Conclusion (2 to 3 minutes)

[*Thank the interviewee.*]

APPENDIX C

EXAMPLE OF SELECTION CRITERIA IDENTIFICATION

IDENTIFYING SELECTION CRITERIA

Store Manager Position

Approach

After the job analysis was done and a job description for hiring purposes was prepared, a group of experts, composed of five regional directors, was brought together to identify the underlying requirements of the store manager position. Individually, each participant had read the job responsibilities and the job context, and then identified the overall requirements for each of the categories. Then the participants did it all again as a group until a consensus was reached. In this example, the group of experts settled on seven knowledge aspects (K), five skills (S), and five other characteristics (O).

The consensus results are presented in Tables C1 and C2. Table C1 shows the underlying requirements for each job responsibility and its context; Table C1 lays out the final selection criteria that were chosen for the store manager position. The requirements identified in step 1 (see Table C1) were not all chosen as selection criteria (see Table C2). The following were eliminated: listening and understanding; consideration for team members; delegation and involvement of others; basic understanding of stock management; and persuasion and negotiation.

Results

Table C1
Requirements according to each responsability domain

RESPONSIBILITIES (TASKS) AND JOB CONTEXT	REQUIREMENTS*
Personalized service (Listens to customers, maintains standards, makes sure products are available and is up-to-date on market trends)	Listening and understanding Customer orientation Monitoring the accomplishment of work and projects Planning and organizing Knowledge of market trends Knowledge of products sold in the store
Staff performance (Establishes a good work atmosphere, manages performance objectives, involves employees, manages employee availability, manages employee development, maintains a safe work environment)	Consideration for team members Monitoring the accomplishment of work and projects Team leadership Involvement of team members Planning and organizing Involvement of others and delegation Basic knowledge of health and safety Knowledge of management principles
Profitability (Does market development, works with the Regional Director, manages resources, manages inventories, manages wages)	Orientation towards action, innovation and risk taking Inclination for teamwork and cooperation Planning and organization Basic knowledge of accounting Basic knowledge of inventory management Ability to use accounting software Ability to use Excel
Community involvement (Joins organizations, creates partnerships according to store needs, encourages and participates in community activities)	Ability to establish networks Persuasion and negotiation Orientation towards action, innovation and risk taking
Job context (Physical, administrative, and psychological environment, technology and equipment)	Monitoring the accomplishment of work and projects Interest in teamwork and cooperation Adaptability and openness to change Pursuit of excellence and success Involvement of team members Team leadership

* The requirements were identified from the inventory presented in Appendix D.

Table C2

Selection criteria for the position of store manager

STORE MANAGER
Technical and professional knowledge (K) 1. Knowledge of market trends 2. Knowledge of the products on sale at the store 3. Basic knowledge of health and safety 4. Knowledge of management principles 5. Basic knowledge of accounting 6. Ability to use the accounting software 7. Ability to use Excel
Skills (S) 1. Planning and organization 2. Team leadership 3. Monitoring the accomplishment of work and projects 4. Involvement of team members 5. Ability to establish networks
Other characteristics (O) 1. Inclination for teamwork and cooperation 2. Orientation towards action, innovation and risk taking 3. Customer orientation 4. Adaptability and openness to change 5. Pursuit of excellence and success

In addition to these selection criteria, the committee members decided on the two following preselection criteria: *a*) a community college diploma, and *b*) two to five years' retail experience, including at least two years in a management position.

APPENDIX D

INVENTORY AND DEFINITIONS OF SELECTION CRITERIA FOR MANAGEMENT POSITIONS

Results-based operational management	
CRITERION 1: Planning and organization	DEFINITION ❖ Uses action plans: clearly defines performance objectives, steps to achieving them, responsibilities and schedules. ❖ Distributes (delegates) the work and responsibilities evenly to the right people based on their skills and abilities. ❖ Gives people the resources they need as well as sufficient authority. ❖ Is appropriately organized: establishes suitable schedules, sets up effective management procedures and systems, is methodical.
CRITERION 2: Monitoring the accomplishment of work and projects	DEFINITION ❖ Keeps daily activities in line with the project's objectives and schedules. ❖ Ensures follow-up and makes corrections if necessary. ❖ Follows budgets and monitors finances. ❖ Evaluates employee performance.
Problem solving and decision making	
CRITERION 3: Problem analysis	DEFINITION ❖ Deals with a large amount of information quickly. ❖ Thinks before acting. ❖ Looks beyond symptoms to find causes. ❖ Gathers and analyzes the data needed for diagnosis. ❖ Develops a group of solutions with their consequences. ❖ Remains objective.
CRITERION 4: Judgment	DEFINITION ❖ Chooses good solutions and makes decisions that are appropriate considering the constraints of the situation. ❖ Always has the company's overall perspective in mind, not just one aspect of it. ❖ Applies policies and procedures with flexibility.
CRITERION 5: Decisiveness and risk taking	DEFINITION ❖ Faces situations firmly, makes difficult decisions and takes unpopular positions when necessary. ❖ Makes decisions whose consequences may be personally disagreeable. ❖ Makes decisions quickly in emergencies, even under pressure. ❖ Intervenes rapidly and immediately when dealing with problems associated with people or their work performance.

	Leadership and team management
CRITERION 6: Team leadership	DEFINITION ❖ Has a desire to lead. ❖ Ensures that all team members have a clear understanding of what they have to do. ❖ Immediately conveys relevant information (decisions, changes, reports, etc.) to the team members who need it. ❖ Gives team members advice (feedback) on their work or responsibilities so that changes can be made as needed.
CRITERION 7: Involvement of others and delegation of major responsibilities	DEFINITION ❖ Explains the reasons for decisions to others. ❖ Consults others regularly about decisions or projects that concern them. ❖ Involves others and allows them to have influence over the decisions concerning them. ❖ Delegates substantial responsibilities and important decisions to others. ❖ Is able to work with subordinates who are clearly identified as experts in their fields without being either too directive or too permissive.
CRITERION 8: Involvement of team members in tasks and projects	DEFINITION ❖ Establishes a work atmosphere that encourages all team members to do their best. ❖ Expresses positive expectations towards team members, encourages them so they feel important and confident of their own abilities. ❖ Sets an example. ❖ Verbally expresses appreciation for a job well done. ❖ Publicly acknowledges team members' achievements.
CRITERION 9: Consideration for team members and their well-being	DEFINITION ❖ Is friendly with team members. ❖ Identifies their needs and makes sure they are met. ❖ Is equitable towards them.
CRITERION 10: Inclination for teamwork and cooperation, conflict resolution	DEFINITION ❖ Recognizes when circumstances require that a job or a decision be handled by a team. ❖ Encourages mutual aid and cooperation, promotes information sharing. ❖ Can coordinate specialists from different fields. ❖ Recognizes conflict situations and settles them effectively.

Interpersonal relations and influence	
CRITERION 11: Listening and understanding	DEFINITION ❖ Listens carefully when talking with people, allows them to speak without cutting them off, even when disagreeing with them. ❖ Puts self in others' shoes during a discussion, in order to try and understand their point of view and feelings.
CRITERION 12: Persuasion and negotiation	DEFINITION ❖ Quickly gains others' confidence. ❖ Negotiates win-win solutions that are fair for all parties. ❖ Can be persuasive while maintaining good relations.
CRITERION 13: Organizational strategy and know-how	DEFINITION ❖ Involves others to achieve objectives. ❖ Takes steps to be well informed. ❖ Builds formal and informal networks of relationships. ❖ Knows who to talk to outside the team or the department when necessary. ❖ Understands the company and how it works. ❖ Can deal with the company's political realities.
Other personal qualities	
CRITERION 14: Pursuit of excellence and success	DEFINITION ❖ Feels the need to excel, to accomplish something unique. ❖ Always wants to do better, be the best. ❖ Perseveres. ❖ Is dynamic, energetic, very hard-working.
CRITERION 15: Orientation towards action, innovation and risk taking	DEFINITION ❖ Is action- and results-oriented. ❖ Is optimistic and feels powerful enough to influence surrounding events. ❖ Takes the initiative to make changes. ❖ Takes risks to seize opportunities that arise.
CRITERION 16: Self-confidence, maturity and emotional control	DEFINITION ❖ Has confidence in self and abilities. ❖ Has emotional self-control. ❖ Can work under stressful conditions. ❖ Is not afraid of responsibility or of taking on a difficult project or situation. ❖ Is able to express disagreement and stick to decisions in the face of opposition or setbacks.

Other personal qualities (continued)	
CRITERION 17: Sense of responsibility, reliability and integrity	DEFINITION ❖ Meets commitments, keeps promises, meets deadlines. ❖ Puts the company's interests above personal interests. ❖ Is concerned about the quality of the work. ❖ Takes full responsibility for his or her actions or decisions. ❖ Acts ethically and morally, no matter what the circumstances. ❖ Treats everyone fairly with no favouritism.
CRITERION 18: Adaptability and openness to change	DEFINITION ❖ Accepts uncertainty and the unexpected. ❖ Adapts planning, approaches, strategies, policies and practices according to the demands of the situation. ❖ Easily accepts changes that arise and adapts to them rapidly (e.g., innovations, technologies, new management approaches). ❖ Welcomes other points of view.
CRITERION 19: Openness to criticism, acceptance of own limitations	DEFINITION ❖ Knows his or her strengths or weaknesses. ❖ Is open to criticism, without being defensive. ❖ Admits errors, does not try to blame others.
CRITERION 20: Customer orientation	DEFINITION ❖ Tries to identify the customers' real needs. ❖ Establishes friendly and professional contact with customers. ❖ Is fully committed to maintaining high quality customer service. ❖ Suggests products, services or solutions appropriate to customers' needs.
CRITERION 21: Ability to develop networks	DEFINITION ❖ Establishes a network of contacts with people working in various sectors of the organization. ❖ Establishes a network of contacts with people working in the same sector of the industry, both inside and outside the company. ❖ Maintains effective relationships with the people in these networks. ❖ Develops a relationship of mutual aid with the people in these networks.

Other personal qualities (continued)	
CRITERION 22: Interest in the job	DEFINITION ❖ Has an intrinsic motivation for the job itself and the activities involved. ❖ Has aspirations and a career plan appropriate to the opportunities offered. ❖ Is attracted by the job conditions (workplace, schedule, salary, etc.).
CRITERION 23: Specialized knowledge	DEFINITION ❖ Has the knowledge and techniques needed for the job.

APPENDIX E

A GUIDE TO DESIGNING SITUATIONAL AND BEHAVIOURAL QUESTIONS

PREAMBLE

The following is a guide to designing situational and behavioural questions. Several approaches are possible, depending on the standardization of questions and responses. Two of these **approaches**, which advocate highly standardized questions and evaluation methods, are suggested as illustrations.

a) The first approach deals with designing questions whose answers are assessed using a high level of standardization: evaluation **by questions** (see *Step 5, Evaluating by Questions*) using the **addition of points** method (see *Step 3, Situational Questions – Evaluating the responses*).

b) The second approach deals with questions whose answers are assessed using a lower level of standardization: evaluation **by criteria** (see *Step 5, Evaluating by Criteria*) using **generic indicators** (see *Step 3, Situational Questions – Evaluating the Responses*).

These two approaches are suitable when the selection context requires a very structured interview. Other approaches, equally valid depending on the selection situation, could have been presented.[1] What follows is a step-by-step description of two ways to design situational and behavioural questions, beginning with situational questions.

DESIGNING SITUATIONAL QUESTIONS

First Approach: Evaluating by Questions Using the Addition of Points Method

Step S1.1

Identify the components from which the situational question will be designed. In most cases, this information will stem from the selection criterion definition or from a critical incident related to the position

1. For example, the evaluation approach using a rating scale composed of real behavioural anchors (Behaviourally Anchored Rating Scale, or BARS) is based on a development process that goes beyond the framework of this volume. Interested readers could consult works that specialize in this area.

to be filled. Other information could be used, such as the job description, material from a training program or already existing situational questions. For the purposes of this exercise, "Customer orientation" (from *Appendix D*) and the first incident from *Appendix B* will be used. This critical incident was chosen because it deals with a situation involving a customer and naturally lends itself to a criterion such as "Customer orientation." Choosing the critical incidents upon which to base the questions is based on judgment.

Example S1.1

Critical incident involving effective behaviour

Situation
A customer asked to see the manager after a purchase he had made from one of the manager's temporary employees. The customer was furious, because the employee had suggested he purchase a product that did not work out for him at all. When he returned to exchange the product, just an hour later, the employee refused to take it back because the seal was broken. The customer pointed out that he had not used the product and reminded the manager that he had been dealing with the store for several years.

Behaviours
The manager first explained that the employee had acted in good faith and was following the company's policies. He said, however, that the employee should have shown more flexibility, given the customer's loyalty to the store. He exchanged the product and gave the customer a good discount on a future purchase. He then met with all his employees to discuss the situation. He authorized the employees to make these kinds of exchanges, but indicated that this type of transaction has to be documented and that any abuse on the part of a customer should be reported to him.

Results
The customer was very satisfied and continued to deal with the company. The employees have greater latitude and little abuse has been noted. The company has acquired a reputation for flexibility that will help increase its customer base.

Definition of the criterion to be measured: "Customer orientation"

- ❖ Tries to identify the customers' real needs.
- ❖ Establishes friendly and professional contact with customers.
- ❖ Is fully committed to maintaining high quality customer service.
- ❖ Suggests products, services or solutions appropriate to customers' needs.

Step S1.2

Write a question based on the components chosen in the preceding step. Usually, this means to recapitulate in the form of a question the main components described under the "Situation" heading of the critical incident. If there are no critical incidents, a situation must be created using other sources of information mentioned in Step S1.1.

Example S1.2

Situational question
A customer asks to see you after making a purchase from one of your temporary employees. The customer was furious, because the employee had suggested he purchase a product that did not work out for him at all. When he returned to exchange the product, just an hour later, the employee refused to take it back because the seal was broken. The customer points out that he has not used the product and reminds you that he has been dealing with the store for several years. What would you do in this situation?

Step S1.3

Make sure that the question covers all aspects of the definition of the criterion to be measured (or all aspects considered relevant to this question) and change the question as needed. This step is based on reasoning and is carried out systematically for each aspect of the criterion. Let's do the exercise for all four aspects of "Customer orientation".

Example S1.3A

a) *Tries to identify the customers' real needs.* The question refers to the customer's needs when it mentions that the employee *"had suggested he purchase a product that did not work out for him at all."* However, the reference could be made even more explicit by rephrasing it this way: *"The customer is furious, because the employee had suggested a product that did not respond to his needs at all."* A good candidate should then be able to pick up on the fact that the customer's needs were not identified correctly and that he has to correct the situation.
b) *Establishes friendly and professional contact with customers.* The question points out that *"the customer is furious,"* which refers to the aspect of establishing friendly contact with the customer. However, the professional part of the contact is less obvious, and candidates would not necessarily deal with that aspect. To make sure it is addressed, the question could be changed to this: *"According to the customer, the salesperson lacked professionalism because he did not take into account the fact that the customer did not use the product."*

Example S1.3A (continued)

c) *Is fully committed to maintaining high quality customer service.* The question reports on a customer's complaint about inadequate service. We can consider that this aspect of the criterion to be measured is appropriately covered by the question. No change is necessary.
d) *Suggests products, services or solutions appropriate to customers' needs.* This aspect is adequately covered by the question, which refers to a product that does not meet the customer's needs. No change is necessary.

After this analysis, the question is modified as follows:

Example S1.3B

Situational question
A customer asks to see you after making a purchase from one of your temporary employees. The customer is furious, because the employee had suggested he purchase a product that did not respond to his needs at all. When he returned to exchange the product, just an hour later, the employee refused to take it back because the seal was broken. According to the customer, the salesperson lacked professionalism because he did not take into account the fact that the customer did not use the product. The customer reminds you that he has been dealing with the store for several years. What would you do in this situation?

In this example, few changes are necessary. This is often the case when critical incidents are well done, complete and relevant to the criterion to be evaluated. In addition, it is not essential that a situational question touch on every aspect of the criterion. The important thing is that the interview questions overall allow candidates to demonstrate their qualifications in relation to all aspects of the criterion.

Step S1.4

Draw up a preliminary list of expected responses or "indicators." (See *Step 2*.) This step deals primarily with gathering the information for the "behaviours" part of the critical incident, which can then be rewritten in the form of expected responses.

Example S1.4

Behaviours from the critical incident	Rewritten as expected responses*
"The manager first explained that the employee had acted in good faith and was following the company's policies."	Explain to the customer that the employee acted in good faith.
	Point out to the customer that the company has policies that must be respected.
"He said, however, that the employee should have shown more flexibility, given the customer's loyalty to the store. "	Apologize to the customer (e.g., indicating that the employee should have shown more flexibility).
	Tell the customer that customers who regularly buy merchandise from the store are very much appreciated.
"He exchanged the product and gave the customer a good discount on a future purchase."	Agree to accommodate the customer (i.e., exchange the product).
	Exceed the customer's expectations (e.g., offer him a good discount).
"He then met with all his employees to discuss the situation. He authorized the employees to make these kinds of exchanges."	Give more latitude to employees so they can respond to customers' needs (e.g., allowing them to make exchanges).
"But he indicated that this type of transaction has to be documented and that any abuse on the part of a customer should be reported to him."	This statement clarifies a response component that has already been written (i.e., Agree to accommodate the customer). The response could be further rewritten to read: Agree to accommodate the customer when the request is reasonable (e.g., by exchanging the product, if there has been no abuse).

* The expected response components suggested in this and the following examples are merely illustrations and should not be considered as absolutes.

Step S1.5

Augment the preliminary list of expected responses, taking into consideration the various aspects of the definition of the criterion to be measured. This step is two-fold. First, the expected responses established in Step S1.4 must be grouped under each aspect of the criterion definition. Then these expected responses will be completed with additional responses to adequately cover all aspects of the criterion.

Example S1.5

Aspects of the criterion to be measured	1. Classification of expected responses (from Step 4)	2. Additional expected responses
Tries to identify the customers' real needs.		Clearly identify customers' needs.
Establishes friendly and professional contact with customers.	Explain to the customer that the employee acted in good faith.	
	Point out to the customer that the company has policies that must be respected.	
	Apologize to the customer (e.g., indicating that the employee should have shown more flexibility).	
	Tell the customer that customers who regularly buy merchandise from the store are very much appreciated.	
Is fully committed to maintaining high quality customer service.	Agree to accommodate the customer (i.e., exchange the product if there has been no abuse).	
	Exceed the customer's expectations (e.g., offer him a good discount).	
	Give employees more latitude so they can respond to customers' needs (e.g., allow them to make exchanges).	
Suggests products, services or solutions appropriate to customers' needs.		Suggest a product that responds to the needs identified by the customer.

In this example, we note that none of the response components from Step S1.4 touch on the first aspect of the criterion, *"Tries to identify the customers' real needs,"* therefore the response *"Clearly identify customers' needs"* is added. Similarly, the response *"Suggest a product that responds to the needs identified by the customer"* is added for the fourth aspect of the criterion, *"Suggests products, services or solutions appropriate to the customers' needs."*

STEP S1.6

If nobody who knows the job well (people called job experts or subject matter experts [SMEs]) played a part in preparing the questions and the evaluation guide, this material must be submitted to SMEs for any changes needed to accurately reflect the job in question and its context. This is the basis for the validity of the questions and the evaluation sheet. These experts, or others, must then assign the point value for each of the expected response components. In the following example, the maximum number of points for the question is 20.[2] Finally, when feasible, testing the questions with a group of people who are representative of the possible candidates is always recommended.

Example S1.6

Situational question
A customer asks to see you after making a purchase from one of your temporary employees. The customer is furious, because the employee had suggested he purchase a product that did not respond to his needs at all. When he returned to exchange the product, just an hour later, the employee refused to take it back because the seal was broken. According to the customer, the salesperson lacked professionalism because he did not take into account the fact that the customer did not use the product. The customer reminds you that he has been dealing with the store for several years. What would you do in this situation?

2. In this example, there is no negative correction; all the response components retained were considered effective. Should we add ineffective response components, or assign them a negative point value? Practitioners do not agree on this issue. Some say yes; others refuse to accept any negative correction. However, from a strict psychometric point of view, we believe that a negative correction is not only possible but also probably more valid. Indeed, which of two candidates is more competent, the one who only gives effective response components, or the one who also gives ineffective response components?

Example S1.6 (continued)

	Expected response components	Point value
1	Clearly identify customers' needs.	5
2	Explain to the customer that the employee acted in good faith.	1
3	Point out to the customer that the company has policies that must be respected.	1
4	Apologize to the customer (e.g., indicating that the employee should have shown more flexibility).	2
5	Tell the customer that customers who regularly buy merchandise from the store are very much appreciated.	1
6	Agree to accommodate the customer (i.e., exchange the product if there has been no abuse).	3
7	Exceed the customer's expectations (e.g., offer him a good discount).	2
8	Give employees more latitude so they can respond to customers' needs (e.g., allow them to make exchanges).	3
9	Suggest a product that responds to the needs identified by the customer.	2
	Total	20

Second Approach: Evaluating by Criteria Using Generic Indicators

Step S2.1

Identify the components that will be the basis for the situational questions. In contrast to the first approach, where the evaluation deals with the responses to one question at a time, evaluation by criteria is an approach whereby the evaluation applies to all the response components relevant to a given selection criterion, no matter how many questions are asked to obtain them. Using this approach, a question may apply to one selection criterion at a time, or several criteria. You must ensure, however, that the questions as a whole will allow measurement of all criteria.

The same sources used previously can provide the components for the situational questions: critical incidents, selection criteria definitions, the job description, material from a training program, etc. As an illustration, two critical incidents (the third example of effective behaviour and the first example of ineffective behaviour from *Appendix B*) will be used, but will only be dealt with in relation to a single criterion, "Orientation towards action, innovation and risk taking" (from *Appendix D*). These critical incidents were chosen because the situations involved are relevant to the criterion being evaluated.

Example S2.1

Critical incident involving an effective behaviour
Situation A member of a local association contacted the manager about getting a demonstration on natural products. Only one date was possible, and the manager already had a personal activity planned for that date. The local association had been created just a year or so before, and was mostly made up of young people, a clientele that is not strongly inclined to use natural products. **Behaviours** The manager hesitated at first, but in the end decided to make the presentation at the requested time. He put off his personal appointment. Then he contacted the president of the association to find out about the members' needs. He prepared promotional material and distributed it to the participants. **Results** The manager's presentation was a success. The members of the association volunteer their services to seniors living at home. They gave the seniors the pamphlets, and the seniors began using the natural products. The presentation helped the manager increase his customer base. He also established favourable links with several members of the association.
Definition of the criterion to be measured: **"Orientation towards action, innovation and risk taking"**
❖ Is action- and results-oriented. ❖ Is optimistic and feels powerful enough to influence surrounding events. ❖ Takes the initiative to make changes. ❖ Takes risks to seize opportunities that arise.

Example S2.1 (continued)

Critical incident involving an effective behaviour
Situation The company responsible for cleaning the building declared bankruptcy. This company used to wash the floors and windows three times a week, and its bankruptcy happened during one of the store's busiest times. **Behaviours** In order to increase profits by reducing maintenance costs, the manager asked employees to take turns cleaning the store's floors and windows. He set up schedules, bought the necessary equipment and showed an example by doing the job himself once every two weeks. **Results** This decision created general discontent among the employees, who told the manager they had not been hired to do the cleaning. They did the work grudgingly and the store's cleanliness suffered as a result. Two temporary employees quit because of this decision. The manager had to hire and train new staff, which cost him much more than the amount he saved on cleaning. After this experience, he subcontracted the cleaning to another specialized firm.
Definition of the criterion to be measured: "Orientation towards action, innovation and risk taking"
❖ Is action- and results-oriented. ❖ Is optimistic and feels powerful enough to influence surrounding events. ❖ Takes the initiative to make changes. ❖ Takes risks to seize opportunities that arise.

Step S2.2

Formulate the questions on the basis of the components chosen in the preceding step. In the case of critical incidents, this means to rewrite as a question the main elements described under the "Situation" heading.

Example S2.2

Situational question A
The president of a local association contacts you and asks you to make a presentation on natural products to the members of the association. He gives you a date for the presentation. You see that you already have a personal activity planned, but there is no other possible date for the presentation. You know that the association was created just a year or so ago, and is primarily made up of young people, a clientele that is not strongly inclined to use natural products. What would you do in this situation?

Example S2.2 (continued)

Situational question B
You learn that the company that cleaned the building has declared bankruptcy. This company was responsible for washing the store's floors and windows three times a week, and its bankruptcy has happened during one of the store's busiest times. What would you do in this situation?

Step S2.3

Make sure that the questions cover all aspects of the definition of the criterion to be measured (or all aspects considered relevant for these questions). This step is based on reasoning, and is carried out systematically for each part of the criterion. We will walk through the exercise for each of the four aspects of the criterion "Oriented toward action, innovation, and risk taking."

Example S2.3A

a) *Is action- and results-oriented.* Question B requires that action be taken to rectify the situation and concrete solutions be suggested to ensure cleanliness of the premises. The "orientation towards action" aspect is covered appropriately. However, neither of the two questions specifically deals with "results-oriented." To correct this, the following sentence could be added to question A: "*You also know that your quarterly sales objectives have not been reached and that your boss has indicated the importance of increasing the customer base at your store.*"
b) *Is optimistic and feels powerful enough to influence surrounding events.* Question A indicates that the local association was created just a year ago, and that it is primarily made up of young people, a clientele not very strongly inclined to use natural products. Good candidates will take the opportunity to say that they are optimistic about the possibility of influencing the audience and convincing young people to buy natural products. We can therefore consider that this aspect of the criterion to be measured is covered.
c) *Takes the initiative to make changes.* Questions A and B both require that changes be made in order to resolve the situation. However, the "change" aspect is not sufficiently explicit. The following sentence could be added to question B to make it more obvious that changes need to be made to the way things are done: *"This is the third time in two years that this has happened, and you think it is partly due to the fact that your company always deals with suppliers who offer the lowest-cost service."*
d) *Takes risks to seize opportunities when they arise.* The presentation to the local association represents a business opportunity in itself. However, the risk-taking aspect could be emphasized by adding the following to question A: *"Preparing the presentation may take a great deal of your time, since you are less familiar with the advantages and disadvantages of these products in relation to this age group."*

After this analysis, the questions are amended and become the following:

Example S2.3B

Situational question A*
The president of a local association contacts you and asks you to make a presentation on natural products to the members of the association. He gives you a date for the presentation. You see that you already have a personal activity planned, but there is no other possible date for the presentation. You know that the association was created just a year or so ago, and is primarily made up of young people, a clientele that is not strongly inclined to use natural products. Preparing the presentation risks taking a great deal of your time, since you are less familiar with the advantages and disadvantages of these products in relation to this age group. You also know that your quarterly sales objectives have not been reached and that your boss has indicated the importance of increasing the clientele at your store. What would you do in this situation?
Situational question B
You learn that the company that cleaned the building has declared bankruptcy. This company was responsible for washing the store's floors and windows three times a week, and its bankruptcy has happened during one of the store's busiest times. This is the third time in two years that this has happened, and you think it is partly due to the fact that your company always deals with suppliers who offer the lowest-cost service. What would you do in this situation?

* To include all the aspects of the criterion to be measured, it is sometimes necessary to use long questions such as this one, which can complicate the candidate's task from the point of view of memorization. To make this less inconvenient, a paper copy of the questions can be provided.

STEP S2.4

Draw up a preliminary list of expected response components. Compared to the previous approach (evaluating by questions with point totalling), these components should be more general in nature (i.e., less specific with regard to the content of each question). They should be sufficiently broad to include candidates' responses to all the questions asked to evaluate this selection criterion.

The information under the "behaviours" heading of the critical incidents retained in Step S2.1 may be very useful. It should be rewritten in terms of general expected response components.

Example S2.4

Behaviours from the critical incidents	Rewritten as expected responses
Critical incident 1 (positive): He hesitated at first, but finally decided to make the presentation at the appointed time.	Acts in spite of the constraints of the situation.
Critical incident 1 (positive): He postponed his personal activity.	Makes compromises to achieve anticipated results.
Critical incident 1 (positive): He contacted the president of the association to find out more about the needs expressed by the members.	Gathers the information needed to resolve the problem effectively.
Critical incident 1 (positive): He prepared promotional material that he distributed to the participants.	Takes advantage of opportunities offered to promote the products and services offered by his company.
Critical incident 2 (negative): He asked his employees to take turns washing the store's floors and windows.	Uses the resources at his disposal appropriately.
Critical incident 2 (negative): He showed an example by taking a turn himself once every two weeks.	Gets involved in activities that have value added for the company.
Critical incident 2 (negative): To increase profits by reducing maintenance costs... he set up schedules, bought the necessary equipment.	Does what is necessary to achieve anticipated results.

As there are no point values and no possibility of a negative correction, the expected response components are usually set up as effective behaviours or positive responses. Therefore, the ineffective behaviours from the negative critical incidents must be transformed into positive responses. For example, the behaviour "*He asked his employees to take turns washing the store's floors and windows*" demonstrates that the manager did not use the resources at his disposal appropriately. He asked the sales staff to perform duties that are usually the job of the housekeeping staff. So this behaviour must be transformed to indicate what should have been done. In the present case, the reformulation takes the following form: "*Uses the resources at his disposal appropriately.*" Obviously, since it is more generic, the response is more subjective.

Step S2.5

Add to the preliminary list of expected responses based on the various aspects of the definition of the criterion to be measured. This step is twofold. First, the expected responses established in Step S2.4 should be grouped according to each aspect of the criterion definition. Second, the expected responses should be completed by adding additional responses to cover all aspects of the criterion.

Example S2.5

Aspects of the criterion to be measured	1. Classification of expected responses (from Step 4)	2. Additional expected responses
Is action- and results-oriented.	Acts in spite of the constraints of the situation.	
	Uses the resources at his or her disposal appropriately.	
	Gets involved in activities that have value added for the company.	
	Does what is necessary to achieve anticipated results.	
Is optimistic and feels powerful enough to influence surrounding events.	Takes advantage of the opportunities he is offered to promote the products and services offered by his company.	
		Shows optimism in the face of challenges.
		Shows the intention of influencing events in his or her favour.
Takes the initiative to make changes.	Gathers the information needed to resolve the problem effectively.	
		Changes the way of doing things in order to solve problems.
Takes risks to seize opportunities when they arise.	Makes compromises to achieve anticipated results.	
		Takes calculated risks in order to seize opportunities that arise.

In this example, we see that only one component touches on the second aspect, "*Is optimistic and feels powerful enough to influence surrounding events.*" So we might add, "*Shows optimism in the face of challenges,*" and "*Shows the intention of influencing events in his or her favour.*" To expand the third aspect, which only has one response component, we could add "*Changes the way of doing things in order to solve problems.*" Finally, the fourth aspect can be strengthened with the addition of: "*Takes calculated risks in order to seize opportunities that arise.*"

The expected responses established in this step become the generic indicators to which we will compare the candidates' actual responses.

Step S2.6

Devise a rating scale that will be used to evaluate the candidates' responses. In accordance with the information in *Step 5, Recommended Rating Scales*, we can use a Likert-type scale with four to six gradations made up of generic components or adjectives. Then all that remains to do is to assemble an evaluation guide composed of *a*) the definition of the criterion and its various aspects, *b*) the generic indicators from the previous step, and *c*) the rating scale, as illustrated in the following table.

Example S2.6

Evaluation guide with generic indicators
On the basis of all the elements provided by the candidate relative to the "Oriented toward action, innovation and risk taking" criterion, fill in the following chart and assign a rating from 1 to 5 using the attached scale.
Oriented toward action, initiative, risk-taking
DÉFINITION ❖ Is action- and results-oriented. ❖ Is optimistic, feels powerful enough to change surrounding events. ❖ Takes the initiative to make changes. ❖ Takes risks to seize the opportunities that arise.

Example S2.6 (continued)

INDICATORS

- ❖ Acts in spite of the constraints of the situation.
- ❖ Uses the resources at his or her disposal appropriately.
- ❖ Gets involved in activities that have value added for the company.
- ❖ Does what is necessary to achieve anticipated results.
- ❖ Takes advantage of the opportunities he or she is offered to promote the products and services offered by his company.
- ❖ Shows optimism in the face of challenges.
- ❖ Shows the intention of influencing events in his or her favour.
- ❖ Gathers the information needed to resolve the problem effectively.
- ❖ Changes the way of doing things in order to solve problems.
- ❖ Makes compromises to achieve anticipated results.
- ❖ Takes calculated risks in order to seize opportunities that arise.
- ❖ Other indicators and observations.

Rating scale	
Excellent 5	The candidate covered the aspects described in the criterion definition in a superior way, and clearly surpassed the requirements for the position.
Very good 4	The candidate covered the aspects described in definition of the criterion very well, and more than adequately met the requirements for the position.
Good 3	The candidate covered the aspects described in the definition of the criterion adequately, and met the requirements for the position.
Poor 2	The candidate left out some of the aspects described in the definition of the criterion, or included some aspects that were negative or inappropriate. The candidate's performance was slightly below the requirements of the position.
Unacceptable 1	The candidate covered few of the aspects described in the definition of the criterion, or included several aspects that were negative or inappropriate. The candidate's performance was clearly inadequate for the requirements of the position.

Step S2.7

If people who know the job well (the SMEs) played no part in drawing up the questions and the evaluation guide, this material must be submitted to them for any changes needed to accurately reflect the job in question and its context. Finally, when feasible, testing the questions with a group of people who are representative of the possible candidates is always recommended.

DESIGNING BEHAVIOURAL QUESTIONS

First Approach: Evaluating by Questions Using a Total Score

STEP B1.1

Identify the aspects that the behavioural question will be based on. This step is identical to Step S1.1 under *Designing Situational Questions*. For the purposes of the exercise, the same critical incident and the same criterion to be evaluated, "Customer orientation," will be used. (See *Example S1.1*.)

STEP B1.2

Design a question based on the aspects from the previous step. The question must establish the context of the behaviour example requested and be at an appropriate level of complexity for the job. As with situational questions, the question can be written using the information under the "Situation" heading in the critical incident or other sources of information. (See Step S1.1.)

Example B1.2

Some customers have been complaining about the quality of the service. Can you give an example of a recent situation in which you had to face a customer who was particularly unhappy with the service received from one of your employees?

STEP B1.3

Write prompting questions that will provide a complete example of behaviour (situation, actions, results) and allow you to evaluate all the aspects of the criterion to be measured. Since behavioural questions have a more general formulation than situational questions, it is important to guide the candidates and give them the opportunity to demonstrate their qualifications. Following are a few examples of prompting questions:

Example B1.3

Situation
- What happened exactly?
- Who was the customer? Was it a new customer? An important one?
- Was it the first time this customer was complaining?
- Who was the employee? Was it a good employee or a problematic one?

Actions
- What exactly did you do?
- What did you tell the customer?
- What did you tell the employee in question?

Results
- What were the consequences of your actions?
- Short-term consequences? Long-term consequences?

Step B1.4

Draw up a preliminary list of expected responses. As with the situational questions, this step is primarily done on the basis of the information in the "Behaviour" part of the critical incident, rewritten as expected responses. In the case of behavioural questions, however, the components of expected responses must be relatively generic, rather than written to correspond closely to the critical incident. Faced with the behavioural questions, the candidates will give examples drawn from their own experience, which is bound to lead to a broad diversity of responses from one candidate to another. Consequently, the expected response components have to be sufficiently general to cover this diversity.

Example B1.4

Behaviours from the critical incident	Rewritten as expected responses
"He explained first of all that the employee had acted in good faith in following company policies."	Maintains uniform and fair customer service (e.g., respects the company's policies).
	Encourages professionalism of his staff and his company.
"He said, however, that the employee should have shown more flexibility, given the customer's loyalty to the store."	Apologizes to the customer when necessary.
	Shows appreciation for regular customers.

Example B1.4 (continued)

Behaviours from the critical incident	Rewritten as expected responses
"He exchanged the product and gave the customer a good discount on a future purchase."	Shows flexibility towards the customer.
	Surpasses the customers' expectations.
"He then met with all his employees to discuss the situation. He authorized the employees to make these kinds of exchanges."	Implements conditions leading to better customer service.
"But he indicated that this type of transaction has to be documented and that any abuse on the part of a customer should be reported to him."	Maintains uniform and fair customer service (e.g., complies with the company's policies).

Naturally the expected response components must be relevant to the criterion to be evaluated. Thus the first behaviour from the critical incident, "*He explained first of all that the employee had acted in good faith in following company policies,*" gives rise to the expected response "*Maintains uniform and fair customer service (e.g., complies with the company's policies,)*" because of its close relationship to the "Customer orientation" criterion. With a different criterion to evaluate, the same critical incident behaviour would have produced a different response component. For measuring the criterion "Persuasion and negotiation," for example, the response could be "Provides explanations that persuade the customer of the company's good faith," to cover the "Can be persuasive while maintaining good relations" aspect of the definition. (See *Appendix D.*) It is not always possible to transpose each behaviour described in a critical incident into an expected response. The behaviour may sometimes not be relevant to the criterion being measured.

Step B1.5

Add to the preliminary list of expected responses based on the various aspects of the definition of the criterion to be measured. As with the situational questions, this step is twofold. First, the expected responses that were determined in Step B1.4 must be grouped under each of the aspects of the criterion definition. Second, the expected responses must be completed by adding responses to cover all the aspects of the criterion. In the following example, three response components have been added.

Example B1.5

Aspects of the criterion to be measured	1. Classification of expected responses	2. Expected responses added
Tries to identify the customers' real needs.		Identifies the customer's real needs.
Establishes friendly and professional contact with customers.	Maintains uniform and fair customer service (e.g., complies with the company's policies).	Establishes friendly contact with the customer.
	Contributes to the professionalism of his staff and his company.	
	Apologizes to the customer when necessary.	
	Shows appreciation for regular customers.	
Is fully committed to maintaining high quality services for customers.	Shows flexibility towards the customer.	
	Surpasses the customers' expectations.	
	Implements conditions leading to better customer service.	
Suggests products, services or solutions appropriate to customers' needs.		Suggests products, services or solutions appropriate to the customer's needs.

Step B1.6

If it has not already been done, have the main question, the prompting questions and the expected responses looked at by people who know the job well and make changes if needed to accurately reflect the job in question and its context. These experts, or others, must then determine the point value for each of the expected response components. In the following example, this question is worth a maximum of 20 points.

Finally, when feasible, testing the questions with a group of representative people (i.e. from the applicant pool) is always recommended.

Example B1.6

Behavioural question		
Some customers have been complaining about the quality of the service. Can you give an example of a recent situation in which you had to face a customer who was particularly unhappy with the service received from one of your employees? **Situation** • What exactly happened? • Who was the customer? Was it a new customer? An important one? • Was it the first time this customer was complaining? • Who was the employee? Was it a good employee or a problematic one? **Actions** • What exactly did you do? • What did you tell the customer? • What did you tell the employee (or employees) in question? **Results** • What were the consequences of your actions? • Short-term consequences? Long-term consequences?		
	Expected response components	**Points**
1	Identifies the customer's real needs.	3
2	Maintains uniform and fair customer service (e.g., complies with the company's policies).	1
3	Establishes friendly contact with the customer.	3
4	Contributes to the professionalism of his staff and his company.	1
5	Apologizes to the customer when necessary.	1
6	Shows appreciation for regular customers.	1
7	Shows flexibility towards the customer.	1
8	Surpasses the customers' expectations.	3
9	Implements conditions leading to better customer service.	3
10	Suggests products, services or solutions appropriate to the customers' needs.	3
	Total	20

Second Approach: Evaluation by Criteria with Generic Indicators

Step B2.1

Identify the components upon which the behavioural questions will be based. This step is identical to the one described for designing situational questions: the evaluation applies to all the response components relevant to a given critical incident, no matter how many questions are asked to obtain them. For the purposes of the exercise, the same critical incidents and the same criterion to be evaluated, "Orientation towards action, innovation and risk-taking," will be used. (See Example S2.1.)

Step B2.2

Formulate the questions based on the components chosen in the previous step. The question must establish the context for the requested examples of behaviour and have a level of complexity commensurate with the job. As with the situational questions, these questions may be written using the information under the "Situation" heading in critical incidents, or other sources of information. (See Step S1.1.)

Example B2.2

Behavioural question A
Store managers sometimes have to deal with requests that encroach on their personal time. Can you give an example where you had to choose between an important job and going ahead with a personal activity that you had planned?
Behavioural question B
Store managers have to rely on the cooperation of several suppliers in order to offer quality service to their customers. Can you tell us about a situation where one of your suppliers let you down at a critical moment?

Step B2.3

Formulate prompting questions that will trigger complete examples of behaviours (situation, actions, results) and lend themselves to an overall evaluation of the criterion definition to be measured. Given that behavioural questions are more general than situational questions, it is important to guide the candidates and give them the opportunity to demonstrate their qualifications. Following are a few examples of prompting questions:

Examples B2.3

Example for Question A
Situation • What was the request? • How did it encroach on your personal time? • What was the job you had to accomplish? **Actions** • What exactly did you do? • How did you respond to the request? **Results** • What were the consequences of your actions? In the short term? In the long term? • What was the impact on the personal activity you had planned?
Example for Question B
Situation • What exactly did the supplier do? • To what extent did the services provided by the supplier affect the quality of customer service? • Why did your supplier let you down? **Actions** • What exactly did you do? • What did you say to the supplier? • What steps did you take in the short, medium and long term? **Results** • What were the consequences of your actions? In the short term? In the long term?

Step B4

Draw up a preliminary list of expected response components. This step is identical to Step S2.4; the expected responses must be sufficiently general to include the candidates' responses to all the questions asked in order to evaluate the selection criterion targeted (see Example S2.4).

Step B2.5

Augment the preliminary list of expected response components based on the various aspects of the definition of the criterion to be measured. This step is identical to Step S2.5 (see Example S2.5).

Step B2.6

Devise a rating scale that will be used to evaluate the candidates' responses, then put together an evaluation guide composed of *a)* the definition of the criterion and its various aspects, *b)* the generic indicators from Step B2.5, and *c)* the rating scale. This step is identical to Step S2.6 (see Example S2.6).

Step B2.7

If it has not already been done, have the main question, the prompting questions and the expected responses looked at by people who know the job well and who will make changes if needed to accurately reflect the job in question and its context. When feasible, testing the questions with a group of people representative of the possible candidates is strongly recommended.

APPENDIX F

EXERCISE ON PREPARING SITUATIONAL AND BEHAVIOURAL QUESTIONS

OBJECTIVES

To practise preparing situational and behavioural interview questions, as well as an evaluation guide.

INSTRUCTIONS

The "Planning and organization" and "Judgment" criteria have been chosen for selecting the candidates for a store manager's position (whose job description for selection purposes appears in *Appendix A*). Your task is to design interview questions for each of these criteria following the approaches discussed in *Appendix E, A Guide to Designing Situational and Behavioural Questions*).

Questions for the "Planning and organization" criterion, evaluated by questions with an evaluation guide using addition of points approach

Design **one** situational question and **one** behavioural question to measure the "Planning and organization" criterion. These questions must be drawn up in relation to an evaluation by question with addition of points approach (see *Appendix E*). Formulate the questions based on a critical incident, such as the second example of effective behaviour from *Appendix B*, as follows:

<table>
<tr><th colspan="2">Second example of effective behaviour</th></tr>
<tr><th>Situation</th><th>Result</th></tr>
<tr><td>The Regional Director told the manager that all the stores in the chain had to participate in a promotion campaign to market a new line of natural products. He stressed the importance of this campaign, because the new products were being made by one of the company's subsidiaries.</td><td rowspan="3">The campaign was a complete success and the store had the best sales figures in the district. The exercise was stimulating for the employees, who were motivated by the challenge. The employee presentations have continued and now deal with other products sold in the store.</td></tr>
<tr><th>Behaviour</th></tr>
<tr><td>First of all the store manager gathered all the information about the promotion campaign (dates, types of products, characteristics, etc.). Then he organized a meeting for the employees and asked each of them to make suggestions. After the meeting, every employee was responsible for becoming an expert on one of the new products. They each made a presentation to the other employees. Merchandise in the store was moved in order to place the new products in the best locations. Promotional posters were put up and advertising flyers were distributed to customers. Everyone was ready when the new products arrived.</td></tr>
</table>

The four aspects of "Planning and organization" (defined in *Appendix D*) which must be measured by the interview questions are the following:

Planning and organization
❖ Uses action plans: clearly defines performance objectives, steps to achieving them, responsibilities and schedules. ❖ Distributes the work and responsibilities (delegates) evenly to the right people based on their skills and abilities. ❖ Gives people the resources they need and adequate authority. ❖ Is adequately organized: establishes suitable schedules, sets up effective management procedures and systems, is methodical.

Questions for the "Judgment" criterion, evaluated by criteria using an evaluation guide with generic indicators

Formulate **two** situational questions and **two** behavioural questions to measure the "Judgment" criterion. These must be drawn up in relation to an evaluation by criterion with generic indicators (see *Appendix E*). Base the questions on two critical incidents, the second and third examples of ineffective behaviour from *Appendix B*, as follows:

Second example of ineffective behaviour	
Situation	**Result**
One of the manager's part-time employees, who was a computer science student at the university, suggested that he purchase some specialized stock-management software.	*Only three weeks after acquiring the software, the temporary employee left the store to take a job with a computer company. The software program was complex and no one knew how to make it work properly. The manager asked the District Director for help, and was informed that software for stock management was going to be installed in his store shortly and that he had to get rid of the software he had bought. The whole thing ended up with a loss of several thousand dollars.*
Behaviour	
The employee convinced the manager that this software would help him increase the store's efficiency and reduce losses due to outdated products. He bought the software program and asked the employee to train the others and supervise the entry of the necessary data.	

<table>
<tr><th colspan="2">Third example of ineffective behaviour</th></tr>
<tr><th>Situation</th><th>Result</th></tr>
<tr><td>One of the manager's employees asked him for a raise so he could buy a new house. Normally, raises are established annually at a fixed rate of 3.5%. The employee, who was due to receive his annual raise, had been working for the company for two years and wanted a 6% raise.</td><td rowspan="3">The employee told his colleagues about his good luck and they were upset. They then told the manager that this kind of action smacked of patronage and they had a right to equal treatment. They threatened to bring in the union. After long negotiations, he agreed to give all employees a 5% raise, including the employee who made the original request. In spite of this bonus, the work atmosphere was negatively affected for several weeks.</td></tr>
<tr><th>Behaviours</th></tr>
<tr><td>The manager agreed to the requested raise in view of the employee's superior performance. However, he specified that it was an exceptional measure which would not be repeated in subsequent years.</td></tr>
</table>

The three aspects of the *Judgment* criterion which must be measured by the interview questions are the following:

Judgment
❖ Chooses good solutions, makes decisions appropriate to the constraints of the situation. ❖ Always has the organization's overall perspective in mind, not just one aspect of it. ❖ Applies policies and procedures with flexibility.

PROPOSED SOLUTIONS

The solutions suggested are but a few examples out of many possible good responses to this exercise. Other questions would be as valid as the ones presented here. The expected responses and their point values are also suggested as illustrations; they are not appropriate for use in any particular organization without adaptations.

Questions for the "Planning and organization" criterion, evaluated by questions with addition of points approach		
Situational question		
You are the manager of a store that sells natural products. Your boss tells you that you have to run a promotion campaign to introduce a new line of natural products. He says that expectations are high and you will be expected to reach established sales objectives. The organization of the campaign is entirely up to you. How will you go about planning and organizing the campaign, considering that your four full-time and three part-time employees have very diverse skills and experience?		
Response components		**Points**
1	Gather all the information about the promotion program (dates, product type, characteristics, etc.).	10
2	Define the performance objectives clearly.	10
3	Establish a clear schedule.	10
4	Ask employees to make suggestions about how to conduct the campaign.	10
5	Clearly establish the necessary steps to achieve goals (exactly what must be done).	10
6	Identify employees' strengths and weaknesses.	10
7	Delegate the work on the basis of employees' skills, abilities and availability.	10
8	Make sure to provide employees with appropriate training about the products.	10
9	Make sure to provide all the materiel necessary (e.g., brochures, price lists, etc.).	10
10	Plan periodic evaluations of sales volumes and other effectiveness criteria.	10
	Total	100

Behavioural question
Sometimes our boss may ask us to take on difficult assignments that require a great deal of planning and organization. Can you give a recent example of a situation in which you had to plan and organize a relatively complex project or difficult assignment? **Situation** • What was the nature of this project or assignment? • What made it difficult? • Who was involved, other than your boss and your employees? **Actions** • What did you do exactly? • What was your employees' role in carrying out the project or assignment? • How did you overcome the difficulties that came with it? • What was the easiest thing to accomplish? The most difficult? **Result** • What were the consequences of your actions? • Was the project completed within the established deadlines? If not, why not?

	Response components	Points
1	Knew enough to gather all the relevant information before proceeding.	10
2	Clearly defined the performance objectives.	10
3	Clearly established the schedule.	12
4	Asked employees for suggestions.	12
5	Clearly established the necessary steps to achieve goals (exactly what had to be done).	10
6	Delegated the work on the basis of employees' skills, abilities and availability.	12
7	Gave employees the appropriate training.	10
8	Provided all the material needed to complete the project.	12
9	Planned or carried out periodic evaluations of sales volumes and other effectiveness criteria.	12
	Total	100

Questions for the "Judgment" criterion, evaluated by criteria using generic indicators
First situational question (Question 1)
One of your part-time employees, a computer science student at the university, suggests that you purchase some specialized software that will allow you to manage your inventory better. Currently your store has no such software. What do you do?
Second situational question (Question 2)
You are supervising a group of six people. One of your good employees asks you for a raise so he can buy a house. According to company policy, raises are set annually at a rate of 3.5%. The employee, who is due to receive his annual raise, has been working at the store for two years and wants a 6% raise. What do you do?
First behavioural question (Question 3)
Sometimes employees make suggestions designed to improve the way we run the company. Implementing these suggestions may involve spending time, money and human resources. Can you give a recent example of a situation in which someone suggested an improvement that would require a sizeable investment on the part of the company, whether in time, money or human resources? **Situation** • What were the circumstances? • Who made the suggestion and what was it? • What were the requirements in time, money or human resources? • Who was involved? **Actions** • What did you do exactly? • What were your reasons for this decision? • What was the easiest thing about making the decision? What was the most difficult? **Result** • What were the consequences of your actions? • Did your initial estimate of time, costs or human resources needed to implement the suggestion prove to be correct? • Was the investment worthwhile for the company? Explain.

Second behavioural question (Question 4)
Sometimes managers have to make difficult decisions about one or more employees. Could you give a recent example of a situation in which you had to make a difficult decision about one or more of your employees, knowing that this decision could have a serious impact on all the staff you supervise? **Situation** • What were the circumstances? • What was the nature of the decision you had to make? • What made the decision difficult? How did it affect the staff as a whole? • Who was involved? **Actions** • What did you do exactly? • What were the reasons for your decision? • What was the easiest thing about your decision? The most difficult? **Result** • What were the consequences of your actions? • What was the reaction of the employees who were directly involved? • How did other staff members react?

Evaluation guide	
Based on all the components provided by the candidate for the "Judgment" criterion, fill in the following chart and assign a score between 1 and 5 using the rating scale below.	
Judgment	
DEFINITION ❖ Chooses good solutions, makes decisions appropriate to the constraints of the situation. ❖ Always has the organization's overall perspective in mind, not just one aspect of it. ❖ Applies policies and procedures with flexibility.	
INDICATORS ❖ Makes decisions based on solid judgment. ❖ Does an exhaustive analysis of the situation before acting or making a decision. ❖ Considers the organization's overall perspective when making a decision. ❖ Considers the constraints of the situation before acting or making a decision. ❖ Makes decisions that take both short- and long-term issues into consideration. ❖ Applies policies and procedures with appropriate flexibility for the problem and the circumstances. ❖ Other indicators and observations.	
Rating scale	
Excellent **5**	The candidate covered the aspects described in the criterion definition in a superior way. He clearly surpassed the requirements for the position.
Very good **4**	The candidate covered the aspects described in the criterion definition very well. He more than adequately met the requirements for the position.
Good **3**	The candidate covered the aspects described in the definition of the criterion adequately. He met the requirements for the position.
Poor **2**	The candidate left out some of the aspects described in the definition of the criterion, or included some aspects that were negative or inappropriate. His performance was insufficient to meet the requirements of the position.
Unacceptable **1**	The candidate covered few of the aspects described in the criterion definition, or included several aspects that were negative or inappropriate. His performance was clearly inadequate for the requirements of the position.

APPENDIX G

EXERCISE ON RECOGNIZING AND OBTAINING A TRUE AND COMPLETE BEHAVIOUR DESCRIPTION IN RESPONSE TO BEHAVIOURAL QUESTIONS

OBJECTIVES

In using behavioural questions, try to:

1. Recognize whether the candidate's response is a description of a **true** behaviour (i.e., whether it deals with precise facts and behaviours, not opinions, feelings, interests or behavioural intentions) and whether the description is **complete** (i.e., whether it describes the situation, the actions and the results.)
2. Use appropriate prompting questions to help the candidate provide a true and complete behaviour description.

INSTRUCTIONS

Below are excerpts of candidates' responses to behavioural questions. Some of these make up complete behaviour descriptions. Others only give partial descriptions: they leave out one or more necessary elements, such as the situation, actions or results. Others are false descriptions, or they express opinions, feelings, interests or intentions, or they describe facts and behaviours too vaguely.

For each of these examples, you have two tasks to carry out:

1. Indicate whether the response is:
   A. a true and complete description,
   B. a false description,
   C. an incomplete description – situation missing,
   D. an incomplete description – actions missing, or
   E. an incomplete description – results missing.

   For some examples, more than one answer may apply.
2. Then, where needed, formulate prompting questions that will obtain a true and complete behaviour description.

1	There was just one occasion when I didn't follow the rules. It happened two months ago. I was in a hurry and I ordered my laptop without first getting authorization from the purchasing department. However, I was careful to precisely determine the characteristics the laptop had to have. I contacted three suppliers and asked them for an estimate. I finally chose a computer that suited my needs with the best value for the dollars spent. Overall, I think I did better than might have been expected from purchasing.	A B C D E
	Prompting questions (if necessary):	
2	I have always been pretty independent. I think all employees ought to have this quality. Otherwise they are always checking with their boss who, more often than not, has other things to worry about. Independence equals efficiency, even if that means that mistakes are made. Omelettes are not made without breaking eggs, and as long as the mistakes are minor and can be fixed, it's better to leave employees with as much leeway as possible. It's very rare that I can't take care of my problems myself. I don't have to consult my boss; I know what I have to do.	A B C D E
	Prompting questions (if necessary):	

3	Two of my employees don't get along very well. They argue when the work is being distributed, they have endless debates during team meetings and they are always belittling each other. This had been going on for several years, but recently the situation has gotten worse. It has reached the point that their bickering is upsetting the other team members. First of all I tried to give them a subtle message in informal discussions. That didn't work. I met with them individually and then both at once. I explained the problem and the impact that their behaviour was having on the other members of the team. I told them that I would be making a note in their files if they didn't shape up immediately. I even told them that they could face even more serious consequences if the situation didn't improve. They agreed to change their ways. Ever since, their behaviour has clearly improved. Of course, the atmosphere is still tense. I keep my eyes open and I don't hesitate to intervene if I notice any lapses on their part. Three of my employees have thanked me for intervening like this.		A B C D E
	Prompting questions (if necessary):		
4	I was on a committee that was responsible for making recommendations to our company's board of directors. In most cases, decisions were made quickly without real debate and once a decision had been made, it was very seldom reversed. On one occasion, though, things happened differently. I'll explain the situation. During one meeting, we adopted a resolution after the committee chair recommended it. I didn't react at the time, even though I had the feeling that there was something wrong with it from a legal standpoint. After the meeting, I analyzed the case law and found decisions that clearly showed that our decision was illegal. I made copies of those decisions and presented them at the next meeting. I can tell you that my intervention gave the committee quite a shock.		A B C D E
	Prompting questions (if necessary):		

<table>
<tr><td rowspan="2">5</td><td colspan="2">Once a year, the municipality makes zoning changes that have to be presented to the community at a public meeting. Each year, this process creates passionate debate, in particular among business people, farmers and environmental pressure groups. As the new development officer, I was responsible for organizing this public meeting to convince residents of the merits of proposed changes to the zoning plan. In addition, my boss told me it was critical that I obtain the public's endorsement at the meeting. That wasn't easy, let me tell you. But in the end, all the proposed changes were accepted by the people at the meeting.
The approach I adopted at the annual meeting was greatly appreciated by everyone, and all the meetings like this have followed that approach ever since.</td><td>A
B
C
D
E</td></tr>
<tr><td>Prompting questions (if necessary):</td><td></td><td></td></tr>
<tr><td rowspan="2">6</td><td colspan="2">As team leader, I am responsible for purchasing. I set up a continuous consultation process with the other team members to ensure there would never be any purchasing problems. First I established an ordering calendar that I distributed to all team members. Everyone knew when the ordering was done and they could plan ahead for their needs.
Two days before the date of the next order, I sent a memo to everyone reminding them to fill out their order forms and send them to me.
Then I looked over all the orders and checked to see if it was possible to combine some of them to get quantity discounts. Overall this procedure allowed me to make sure that we were never short of anything. In addition, the company made substantial savings by combining purchases. My boss was very impressed with what I achieved and they are currently studying whether to extend the procedure to the whole company.</td><td>A
B
C
D
E</td></tr>
<tr><td>Prompting questions (if necessary):</td><td></td><td></td></tr>
</table>

7	When I was called as a witness in a grievance action, I felt as though it was a personal attack on me. It was an important grievance for the organization and the union. They were challenging certain management practices that were deeply rooted in the corporate culture. The human resources director met with me to tell me the extent to which my testimony could have a major impact on the final decision. I was to be called at the beginning of the proceedings, so I didn't have the opportunity to observe the other witnesses before I testified. In general, I hated the experience. I was angry at the union lawyer for wanting to discredit me and I worried about it for months. Now I know that it was not a personal attack on me, and that is just the way the procedure is.		A B C D E
	Prompting questions (if necessary):		
8	Yes, there was an occasion when I did not meet an important deadline. My team was supposed to submit a report to a client on a particular date. A large number of activities had to be completed before we could start writing the report. I was in charge of a telephone survey and organizing interviews with several managers working for the client. To accomplish my task, I had prepared a complete worksheet in which I had broken all the steps down into activities. I had planned out the human and material resources needed. It was a tight schedule, and all team members had been warned about the importance of meeting the deadlines. Unfortunately, I had underestimated how long the interviews would take, because I had assumed the managers would all be available. So we overshot the deadline by about 30%. The client never dealt with us again. However, our schedules are now more realistic and we always take unforeseen circumstances into account when we commit to producing a report for a client.		A B C D E
	Prompting questions (if necessary):		

9	I am at the top of my game when I know other people have failed before me. It stimulates me. I see it as a challenge. In all my jobs, I have had the reputation of being the one who could do the impossible. In fact, I think most people let themselves be stopped by little things: administrative constraints, initial objections from certain people, unexpected delays. I think every project should be approached with some faith in your own abilities and those of others. You need to create the conditions that will allow people to feel that they will be able to accomplish their goals. People's motivation accounts for at least half the success of any business. You have to be persistent and persevere with and against everything. That's why I insist on obtaining the expected results. My leadership is recognized and I have no difficulty getting people to cooperate.		A B C D E
	Prompting questions (if necessary):		
10	I am the one who suggested bringing in the subcontractors on preparing the proposals for clients. The subcontractors have extensive experience in our area. I decide which among them have the best assets for the clients' needs. I contact them and ask them if they are interested in taking part in writing the proposal. Obviously, since we don't have the contract yet, that means their contribution is unpaid. Then we organize meetings during which we exchange ideas and establish an action plan. I am usually responsible for the first draft of the proposal, which I then distribute to everyone for comments. I then modify the proposal based on their suggestions, and write the final proposal, which is then submitted to the client. This way of doing things means we can immediately involve the subcontractors who will have an important role to play in bringing the project to fruition.		A B C D E
	Prompting questions (if necessary):		

PROPOSED SOLUTIONS

The solutions are proposed as illustrations, as a rough guide. In an actual interview context, the interpretation of this kind of response component and the way to react to it depend on the way the interview unfolds and the job in question.

<table>
<tr><td rowspan="2">1</td><td colspan="2">C. Situation missing. We don't know why the person was in a hurry, or why he or she thought it was necessary to go ahead without an authorization from the purchasing department, which prevents the interviewers from understanding and evaluating this action.
E. Results missing. We don't know what the consequences of the action were (e.g., reprimand, getting the computer within the required deadline).</td></tr>
<tr><td>Prompting questions</td><td>❖ Why were you in a hurry? Why did you have to order your laptop so quickly?
❖ Why, in these circumstances, did you decide not to ask for the authorization of the purchasing department?
❖ What were the consequences of not having received authorization from purchasing in advance? What happened afterwards?</td></tr>
<tr><td rowspan="2">2</td><td colspan="2">B. False description. The person has not given a concrete example of a situation that he or she experienced. The interviewer must try again and ask the candidate to describe a real situation.</td></tr>
<tr><td>Prompting questions</td><td>❖ Could you talk about a concrete situation in which you have demonstrated this kind of independence? We would be particularly interested in hearing about the context of this situation, what you did, who was involved and the consequences of your actions.</td></tr>
<tr><td rowspan="2">3</td><td colspan="2">A. True and complete description. The situation, the actions and the results are clearly explained by the candidate. However, you could ask for more details.</td></tr>
<tr><td>Prompting question</td><td>❖ How did you approach the situation with the other employees?</td></tr>
<tr><td rowspan="2">4</td><td colspan="2">E. Results missing. Apart from having shocked the committee, we don't know what the actual consequences of this action were. For example, was the recommendation reversed? How did the chairperson react to the information provided? What were the consequences in the short, medium and long term?</td></tr>
<tr><td>Prompting questions</td><td>❖ Was the recommendation reversed?
❖ How did the chair react to the information provided?
❖ What were the consequences of your intervention in the short, medium and long term?</td></tr>
</table>

5	D. **Actions missing.** We don't know how the candidate set about resolving the situation.	
	Prompting questions	❖ What did you do exactly to convince people to modify the zoning plan? How did you respond to their objections and concerns? What was the approach you took? ❖ How did you succeed in reconciling the divergent positions of the business people, farmers and environmental pressure groups?
6	C. **Situation missing**. We do not know the reasons behind the candidate's actions. What was the context? Why did the person think it was a good idea to put this procedure in place? Was it a follow-up to a request from the boss, or was it personal initiative? In other words, without more information about the situation, we cannot situate the candidate's actions properly.	
	Prompting questions	❖ Why did you think it was a good idea to set up this system? Where did this initiative come from? ❖ Why in particular did you choose the procedure you established?
7	D. **Missing actions.** The response indicates that the candidate reacted emotionally. However, we do not know what he or she actually did to arrive at the conclusion that it was not a personal attack. Nor do we know what the candidate did during the hearings, and what made him or her hate the experience. E. **Missing results.** We do not know what the consequences were, beyond the candidate's awareness that he or she was not targeted personally. Was the candidate's point of view adopted by the arbitrator? Did the candidate participate in other grievances after this one? What were the consequences for the organization?	
	Prompting questions	❖ What did you do exactly during the hearings? ❖ Why did you hate the experience? ❖ What made you come to the conclusion that you were not personally targeted? Did you talk about it with other witnesses, or the lawyer? ❖ What was the impact of your testimony on the arbitrator's decision? What were the consequences of this experience for you? For your organization?
8	A. **True and complete description.** The situation, the actions and the results are explained by the candidate. However, you could ask for more details.	
	Prompting question	❖ How did the members of your team react to the situation? Your boss?

<table>
<tr><td rowspan="2">9</td><td colspan="2">B. False description. The person has not given a concrete example of a situation that he or she experienced.</td></tr>
<tr><td>Prompting questions</td><td>❖ Can you tell us about a concrete situation in which you were stimulated by another person's failure?
❖ What was the nature of this failure? What did you do, exactly?
❖ What were the exact consequences of your actions?</td></tr>
<tr><td rowspan="2">10</td><td colspan="2">C. Situation missing. The context that was the basis for this action has not been described. Why did the candidate think it was necessary to involve the subcontractors when writing the proposal for the clients? Was the organization having trouble getting contracts? Was there a lack of cooperation or synergy among the subcontractors fulfilling the contracts? The information given does not allow us to clearly understand the reasons for the actions.
E. Results missing. The results of the action are not described. Did this approach provide more contracts? Did it ensure more synergy?</td></tr>
<tr><td>Prompting questions</td><td>❖ Why did you think it would be a good idea to involve the subcontractors in writing the proposals? What were the actual circumstances that led you to take this action?
❖ What were the actual consequences of integrating the subcontractors into the preparation of proposals? Were there advantages and disadvantages?</td></tr>
</table>

APPENDIX H

EXERCISE ON MAINTAINING THE STRUCTURE OF THE INTERVIEW AND PRESERVING THE CANDIDATE'S SELF-ESTEEM

OBJECTIVE

Try to apply various techniques to maintain the structure and keep control of the interview, and to maintain the candidate's self-esteem.

INSTRUCTIONS

Below are various excerpts of exchanges between interviewers and candidates.

For each of these excerpts, your task as an interviewer is to react appropriately to get the candidate to answer the initial question.

Remember to follow the general rules governing the formulation of questions and responses.

1	**Criterion evaluated:** Computer programming skills	
	Interviewer: "Can you give me an example of a situation in which you were not able to arrive at a solution on your own, a case that was beyond your competence as a programmer?"	**Candidate:** "No, not really. [After several seconds of silence.] No, I can't think of any, except for some unimportant ones."
	Interviewer:	

<table>
<tr><td>2</td><td colspan="3">Criterion evaluated: Leadership</td></tr>
<tr><td></td><td colspan="2">Interviewer: "The department administration has noted problems with confidentiality of written communication. Corrective measures were therefore announced to all staff. Most employees indicated that they do not agree with them. They think the measures put forward by the administration were inappropriate – they make their work harder without guaranteeing an improvement in confidentiality. They add that it shows the administration was really insensitive to the constraints they are working under. As head of the mail service, what do you do?"</td><td>Candidate: "Well, you know, I was responsible for mail service in the private sector for nearly 12 years, in two different organizations, and I was always able to ensure confidentiality. I can guarantee that I know how to do it. In my two previous jobs, I set up a simple and efficient system that was based on five operating rules. The first was…"</td></tr>
<tr><td></td><td>Interviewer:</td><td colspan="2"></td></tr>
<tr><td>3</td><td colspan="3">Criterion evaluated: Specialized knowledge of the field</td></tr>
<tr><td></td><td colspan="2">Interviewer: "In the department, as in the public service as a whole, we are talking about new human resource management techniques. Explain the advantages of the competency approach compared to the traditional approach to personnel selection."</td><td>Candidate: "I don't understand the question."</td></tr>
<tr><td></td><td colspan="2">Interviewer: Repeats the question</td><td>Candidate: "I'm afraid I don't know much about it." [The person is visibly embarrassed.]</td></tr>
<tr><td></td><td>Interviewer:</td><td colspan="2"></td></tr>
</table>

4	**Criterion evaluated:** Work experience		
	Interviewer: "Tell us briefly about the work experience you have acquired in a support and advisory role that has prepared you for this position in human resource management."		**Candidate:** [After 15 minutes, the candidate is still giving so many details that it seems there will be no end to it.]
	Interviewer:		
5	**Criterion evaluated:** Team spirit		
	Interviewer: "Sometimes it happens that we do not agree with our colleagues on the best way to do something or achieve an objective. Can you tell us about the last time that happened to you and what you did about it?"		**Candidate:** "At the last committee meeting, I was the only one who wanted to maintain the project management training program. The others voted against my proposal and the program was cancelled. In another case, however, on the allocation of the budget, I was able to convince them to support my proposal."
	Interviewer:		
6	**Criterion evaluated:** Organization		
	Interviewer: "Suppose you were Director of Administration and you were asked to implement the business plan that was approved by the authorities. After reading the plan, you note the following: • the plan did not go through a consultation process; • the cost analysis does not seem realistic; and • the schedule is not appropriate for the size of the job. You decide to meet with your superior to suggest some corrections. What would you suggest?"		**Candidate:** "I went through that kind of situation last year. It was a question of meeting with the boss and informing him of the modifications I was suggesting. If he refused them, I would try my best to implement the plan as is. I was not the boss, after all."
	Interviewer:		

PROPOSED SOLUTIONS

The solutions are illustrations, proposed as a rough guide. In an actual interview context, the way you would react to this kind of response depends on the way the interview as a whole unfolds.

1	**Criterion evaluated:** Computer programming skills	
	Interviewer:	Two techniques might be appropriate in this situation. **Insist gently.** "Take a couple of minutes to think about it again. Think of a situation in which that could have happened to you." **OR** **Prior justifications.** "We know that in most cases programmers at your level always end up finding a solution. However, no matter what our level, and I'd be the first to admit it, we have all been faced with problems where we need some help. Take a few more minutes to think about it."
2	**Criterion evaluated:** Leadership	
	Interviewer:	A sequence of two questions might be appropriate in this situation. **Sincere compliments.** "I see that you have a great deal of experience in the field. That's excellent." **FOLLOWED BY** **Redirect the conversation.** "But in the present case, what I'd like to know is how you would specifically approach the situation I just described to you." (Repeat the question if necessary.)
3	**Criterion evaluated:** Knowledge of the field	
	Interviewer:	**If** the terms "competency approach and traditional approach" are part of the competencies measured by the question and should in principle be familiar to the candidate, you could use the following technique: **Insist gently.** "OK. If you are willing, we'll come back to that question at the end of the interview." **If** these terms are not part of the candidate's field and would not necessarily be known by the candidate, you could use the following technique: **Rephrase the question in order to clarify.** "The traditional approach is based on a detailed analysis of each job but the competency approach uses a generic inventory of competences. What would be the advantages of going with this kind of reference list?"

4	**Criterion evaluated:** Work experience	
	Interviewer:	This technique seems most appropriate: **Inform the candidate that time is limited.** "That's interesting, but unfortunately we only have a limited amount of time at our disposal. Could you give us a two-minute summary of the aspects of your professional career that you have not already covered?"
5	**Criterion evaluated:** Team spirit	
	Interviewer:	This technique seems most appropriate: **Ask the candidate to clarify.** "So, you have twice presented a position different from that of the other committee members. Could you give us additional details about these situations? We would be particularly interested in understanding the context of the situations, the precise actions you took and the resulting consequences."
6	**Criterion evaluated:** Organization	
	Interviewer:	This technique seems most appropriate: **Redirect the conversation.** "It's interesting that you have been through a similar situation. But faced with the situation that I just described, what would you do specifically?" (If necessary, repeat the question.)

APPENDIX I

EXERCISE ON DISTINGUISHING BETWEEN A FACT AND AN INTERPRETATION WHEN TAKING NOTES

OBJECTIVE

When taking notes, try to recognize facts and observations and distinguish them from interpretations and judgments.

INSTRUCTIONS

Below are excerpts of notes taken by committee members during selection interviews. Some are facts or observations; others are interpretations or judgments.

Indicate for each of these excerpts whether it is

A. a fact or observation; or

B. an interpretation or judgment.

1	[The candidate] responded correctly to the question.	A. Fact or observation B. Interpretation or judgment
2	[The candidate] has management experience that corresponds to the requirements of the position.	A. Fact or observation B. Interpretation or judgment
3	[The candidate] has a B.Sc. in Agronomy.	A. Fact or observation B. Interpretation or judgment
4	[The candidate] says he has enough knowledge of agronomy.	A. Fact or observation B. Interpretation or judgment
5	[The candidate] says: "Faced with this problem, I would consult my team members as soon as possible, then..."	A. Fact or observation B. Interpretation or judgment
6	[The candidate] is nervous and lacks self-assurance.	A. Fact or observation B. Interpretation or judgment
7	[The candidate] has a very high overall average. His scores are higher than the average for his group.	A. Fact or observation B. Interpretation or judgment
8	[The candidate] responds systematically.	A. Fact or observation B. Interpretation or judgment
9	[The candidate] thinks before answering.	A. Fact or observation B. Interpretation or judgment
10	[The candidate] responds frankly.	A. Fact or observation B. Interpretation or judgment

PROPOSED SOLUTIONS

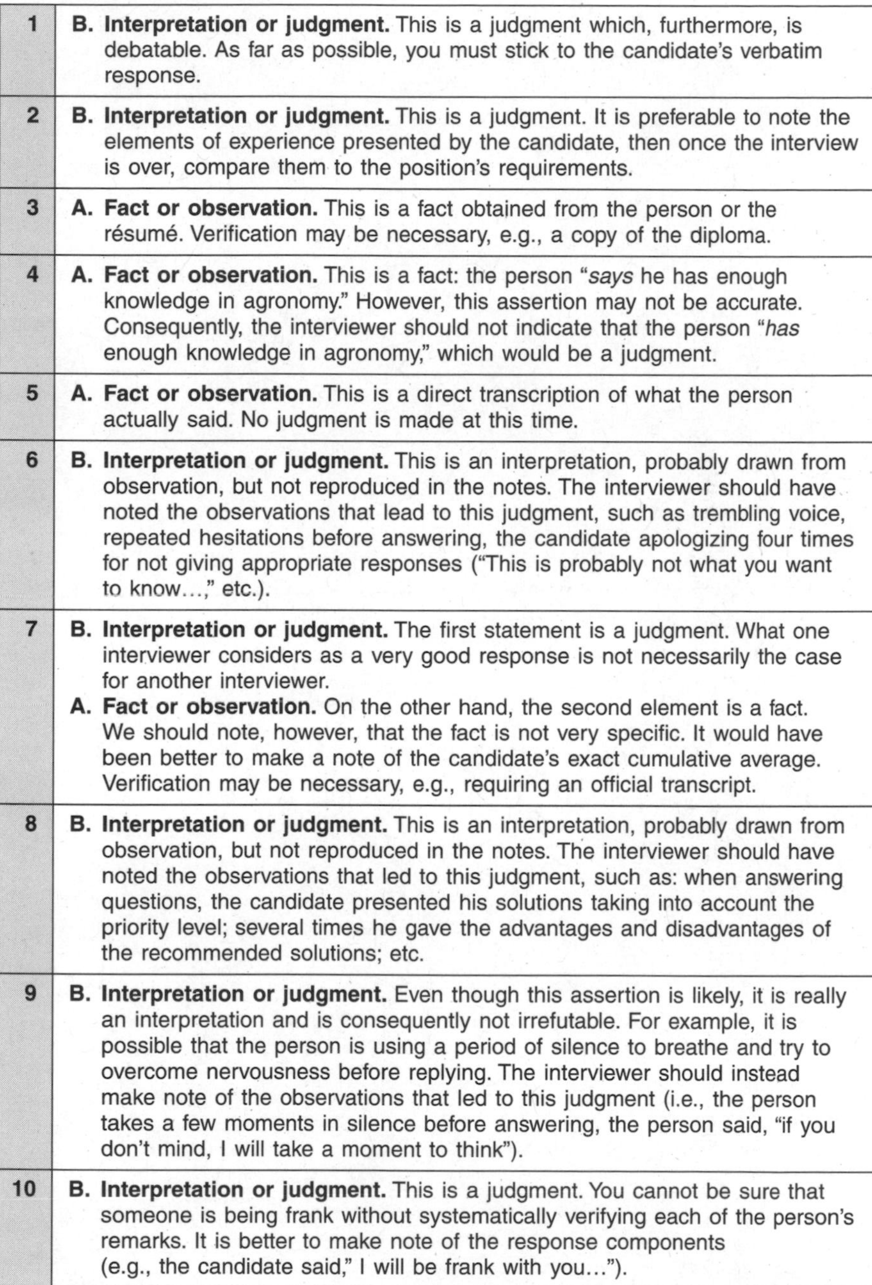

1	**B. Interpretation or judgment.** This is a judgment which, furthermore, is debatable. As far as possible, you must stick to the candidate's verbatim response.
2	**B. Interpretation or judgment.** This is a judgment. It is preferable to note the elements of experience presented by the candidate, then once the interview is over, compare them to the position's requirements.
3	**A. Fact or observation.** This is a fact obtained from the person or the résumé. Verification may be necessary, e.g., a copy of the diploma.
4	**A. Fact or observation.** This is a fact: the person "*says* he has enough knowledge in agronomy." However, this assertion may not be accurate. Consequently, the interviewer should not indicate that the person "*has* enough knowledge in agronomy," which would be a judgment.
5	**A. Fact or observation.** This is a direct transcription of what the person actually said. No judgment is made at this time.
6	**B. Interpretation or judgment.** This is an interpretation, probably drawn from observation, but not reproduced in the notes. The interviewer should have noted the observations that lead to this judgment, such as trembling voice, repeated hesitations before answering, the candidate apologizing four times for not giving appropriate responses ("This is probably not what you want to know…," etc.).
7	**B. Interpretation or judgment.** The first statement is a judgment. What one interviewer considers as a very good response is not necessarily the case for another interviewer. **A. Fact or observation.** On the other hand, the second element is a fact. We should note, however, that the fact is not very specific. It would have been better to make a note of the candidate's exact cumulative average. Verification may be necessary, e.g., requiring an official transcript.
8	**B. Interpretation or judgment.** This is an interpretation, probably drawn from observation, but not reproduced in the notes. The interviewer should have noted the observations that led to this judgment, such as: when answering questions, the candidate presented his solutions taking into account the priority level; several times he gave the advantages and disadvantages of the recommended solutions; etc.
9	**B. Interpretation or judgment.** Even though this assertion is likely, it is really an interpretation and is consequently not irrefutable. For example, it is possible that the person is using a period of silence to breathe and try to overcome nervousness before replying. The interviewer should instead make note of the observations that led to this judgment (i.e., the person takes a few moments in silence before answering, the person said, "if you don't mind, I will take a moment to think").
10	**B. Interpretation or judgment.** This is a judgment. You cannot be sure that someone is being frank without systematically verifying each of the person's remarks. It is better to make note of the response components (e.g., the candidate said," I will be frank with you…").

APPENDIX J

EXERCISE ON ORGANIZING CANDIDATES' RESPONSES ACCORDING TO EVALUATION CRITERIA

OBJECTIVE

To evaluate a candidate, try to group the information provided according to each of the selection criteria measured by the interview.

INSTRUCTIONS

Below you will find a candidate's responses to two questions asked in a selection interview. The questions were drawn up based on an evaluation of the responses by criteria (see *Step 5, Evaluation by Criteria*).

Your task is to organize the relevant response components according to each of the aspects of the following selection criteria:

Team leadership	❖ Has a desire to lead. ❖ Ensures that all team members have a clear understanding of what they have to do. ❖ Immediately conveys relevant information (decisions, changes, reports, etc.) to the team members who need it. ❖ Gives team members advice (feedback) on their work or responsibilities so that changes can be made as needed.
Involvement of team members in tasks and projects	❖ Establishes a work atmosphere that encourages all team members to do their best. ❖ Expresses positive expectations towards team members, encourages them so they feel important and confident of their own abilities. ❖ Sets an example. ❖ Verbally expresses appreciation for a job well done. ❖ Publicly acknowledges team members' achievements.

To make the task easier, the candidate's statements are identified with a number at the beginning of each sentence.

Question 1

The marketing department announces that it has obtained a big contract with a new client. Your boss, who is head of production, meets with you and the other unit heads to divide up the jobs that need to be done for this new contract. From the outset, your colleagues indicate that they are overwhelmed and prefer not to get involved in this venture. You know that the new client has a reputation for being extremely demanding. You also know that your six employees are currently very busy. What do you do?

Candidate's responses

(1) *The first thing to do is to set priorities.* ***(2)*** *What does my boss want?* ***(3)*** *The company?* ***(4)*** *If the contract is important and they want to give the new client good service, they will have to hire new staff.* ***(5)*** *I'm not scared of this kind of job.* ***(6)*** *Just the opposite – give me ten more employees and I can deliver.*

(7) *So let's say that the answer is yes, and my boss tells me that I will be accountable.* ***(8)*** *The first thing to do is to contact the marketing people and get more details on the job that has to be done.* ***(9)*** *When, how, with whom, etc.* ***(10)*** *Then, if possible, I will meet with the client's representative and we'll discuss expectations.* ***(11)*** *I think it is essential that I establish a climate of trust from the beginning.* ***(12)*** *Then I'll negotiate with my boss.* ***(13)*** *How many staff can I have?*

(14) *When I have all the information, I will meet with my employees and sell them the idea.* ***(15)*** *It's an exciting project; everybody will gain from it, we're going to have new staff, etc.* ***(16)*** *People have to see the project as something positive.*
(17) *But beyond selling it, we have to deliver and do it without killing everybody.*

(18) *I will sit down with them and we'll look at the project realistically.*
(19) *We'll divide up the job into clear steps.* ***(20)*** *Then we'll all have a look at what each of the employees has to do right now.* ***(21)*** *I believe in participative management.* ***(22)*** *We'll try, together, to divide up the work, old and new, between the employees, taking into account the new personnel that we are going to add to the team.*

(23) *I go a lot with people's strengths, and I'll tell them,* ***(24)*** *"You are good at doing this or that.* ***(25)*** *So maybe you could take on this or that aspect…"* ***(26)*** *If the person is willing, then off we go.* ***(27)*** *I do this with each of my employees, then we make a plan on paper with the schedules and the follow-ups set out in advance.*

(28) *With all this, I show my employees that I am personally committed to this.*
(29) *If I have to, I will do some of the tasks myself so they can see that it's as important for me as it is for them.*

(30) *I show all this to my boss, then we're ready to go.* ***(31)*** *There's nothing more exciting for me than leading a new project.* ***(32)*** *I don't understand how my colleagues don't leap at the opportunity.* ***(33)*** *It's a total lack of vision.* ***(34)*** *In fact, I'm going to tell them so.* ***(35)*** *But only once the project has been started.*
(36) *Company loyalty means doing what I have to do to make it work.*

Question 2

Sometimes we have to face difficult situations at work. Can you tell us about a situation in which you had difficulty completing a project? In your answer, we would like you to give us the following details:

Situation
- What kind of project was it?
- How was it difficult?
- Who was involved?

Actions
- What did you do exactly?
- How did you overcome the project's difficulties?
- What was the easiest thing to accomplish? The most difficult?

Result
- What were the consequences of your actions?
- Was your project completed to your satisfaction? If not, why not?

Candidate's responses
(37) *I remember one project that was particularly difficult.* ***(38)*** *It wasn't the project itself so much as the circumstances surrounding it.* ***(39)*** *The company was in financial difficulty and management had had to lay some people off, including two of the eight people I was supervising.* ***(40)*** *Morale was at an absolute low.* ***(41)*** *The jobs themselves hadn't changed.* ***(42)*** *We had to get through as much work with fewer people.* ***(43)*** *We still had to finish a big project in a month and we were only in the beginning stages.* ***(44)*** *Everything remained to be done and usually a project like this would take at least six to eight weeks to complete.* ***(45)*** *What I did was to close up shop for a half-day.* ***(46)*** *You'll say that was crazy, but for me, the first job was to get my team together.* ***(47)*** *I invited them to my place for an afternoon and we had a huge barbecue.* ***(48)*** *I looked at my team in the eye and explained the situation.* ***(49)*** *We had these things to do and within this deadline.* ***(50)*** *If we couldn't deliver, we might lose clients.* ***(51)*** *And if we lost clients, there would have to be more layoffs.* ***(52)*** *So either we all had to get on board and roll up our sleeves, or watch the train pull out of the station leaving us behind, jobless.* ***(53)*** *To be honest, it wasn't easy.* ***(54)*** *The employees were very upset and several of them wanted to know why they should work hard for a company that was putting its people out of work.* ***(55)*** *I almost lost the gamble.* ***(56)*** *But Josseline, the young woman on the team who was last hired, saved the day.* ***(57)*** *She told us,* ***(58)*** *"Listen; if we lose clients, I'm the next one to go.* ***(59)*** *I don't want to lose my job.* ***(60)*** *So if you won't do it for the company, do it for me."* ***(61)*** *That seemed to wake everybody up.* ***(62)*** *I have to hand it to Josseline, she's really good at pulling everyone together, because afterwards, she wasn't afraid to take the bull by the horns and work extra hours if need be.* ***(63)*** *From then on, everything went smoothly.* ***(64)*** *I divided up the tasks, we established priorities together, I talked to my boss about it and we succeeded in getting everything done within the deadline.* ***(65)*** *We had to work overtime, but we did it.* ***(66)*** *At the end of the project, I wrote a memo to my boss to point out the exceptional work my employees had done.* ***(67)*** *Since the company didn't have much money, he wasn't able to give out bonuses, but he gave me permission to give everybody a day off.* ***(68)*** *And guess what?* ***(69)*** *We all got together at our place around the barbecue, but this time it was a party and I gave them all a big pat on the back.*

PROPOSED SOLUTIONS

Criterion: Team leadership	
Aspects of the criterion	**Candidate's responses**
Has a desire to lead.	***(5)*** *I'm not scared of this kind of job.* ***(6)*** *Just the opposite – give me ten more employees and I can deliver.* ***(31)*** *There's nothing more exciting for me than leading a new project.*
Ensures that all team members have a clear understanding of what they have to do.	***(19)*** *We'll divide up the job into clear steps.* ***(20)*** *Then we'll all have a look at what each of the employees has to do right now.* ***(21)*** *I believe in participative management.* ***(22)*** *We'll try, together, to divide up the work, old and new, between the employees, taking into account the new personnel that we are going to add to the team.* ***(25)*** *"So maybe you could take on this or that aspect..."* ***(26)*** *If the person is willing, then off we go.* ***(27)*** *I do this with each of my employees, then we make a plan on paper with the schedules and the follow-ups set out in advance.* ***(64)*** *I divided up the tasks, we established priorities together...*
Immediately conveys relevant information (decisions, changes, reports, etc.) to the team members who need it.	***(14)*** *When I have all the information, I will meet with my employees and sell them the idea.* ***(48)*** *I looked at my team in the eye and explained the situation.* ***(49)*** *We had these things to do and within this deadline.* ***(50)*** *If we couldn't deliver, we might lose clients.* ***(51)*** *And if we lose clients, there would have to be more layoffs.* ***(52)*** *So either we all had to get on board and roll up our sleeves, or watch the train pull out of the station leaving us behind, jobless.*
Gives team members advice (feedback) on their work or responsibilities so that changes can be made as needed.	

Criterion: Involvement of team members in tasks and projects	
Aspects of the criterion	**Candidate's responses**
Establishes a work atmosphere that encourages all team members to do their best.	***(15)*** *It's an exciting project, everybody will gain from it, we're going to have new staff, etc.* ***(16)*** *People have to see the project as something positive.* ***(17)*** *But beyond selling it, we have to deliver and do it without killing everybody.* ***(46)*** *... for me, the first job was to get my team together.*
Expresses positive expectations towards team members, encourages them so they feel important and confident of their own abilities.	***(23)*** *I go a lot with people's strengths, and I'll tell them,* ***(24)*** *"You are good at doing this or that."*
Sets an example.	***(28)*** *With all this, I show my employees that I am personally committed to this.* ***(29)*** *If I have to, I will do some of the tasks myself so they can see that it's as important for me as it is for them.*
Verbally expresses appreciation for a job well done.	***(69)*** *... I gave them all a big pat on the back.*
Publicly acknowledges team members' achievements.	***(56)*** *But Josseline, the young woman who was last hired, saved the day.* ***(62)*** *I have to hand it to Josseline, she's really good at pulling people together, because afterwards, she wasn't afraid to take the bull by the horns and work extra hours if need be.* ***(66)*** *At the end of the project, I wrote a memo to my boss to point out the exceptional work my employees had done.*